JAPANESE CERAMICS
of the
LAST 100 YEARS

JAPANESE

CERAMICS
of the
LAST 100 YEARS

by Irene Stitt

CROWN PUBLISHERS, INC., NEW YORK

To my late father
Percy H. Dannatt

I would like to thank the many people who have been so kind and patient with me over my innumerable questions: Dr. Jan Fonteyn of the Museum of Fine Arts, Boston; Louise Cort of the Fogg Art Museum, Cambridge, Massachusetts; Mrs. W. H. Shreve of the Peabody Museum, Salem; Robert Moes and Mrs. Amy Poster of the Brooklyn Museum; Julia Meech of the Metropolitan Museum of Art, New York; J. L. Ayers of the Victoria and Albert Museum, London; Mrs. J. Semal of Japan House, New York; and August Lux, of Lux-Denise Antiques, whose help has been invaluable to me.

My thanks, too, to all those who lent me their treasures to photograph, especially to Mrs. Dae Bade of Lavender and Old Lace, Otto Bade of Remember When, R. Manning and M. Rudin of Orphans of the Attic, Mrs. Lu Walkowski of Mere Pittance, and Jules Wiegel of Wiegel's Nest of Antiques. Also to Mrs. Kathryn Pinney, without whose help and encouragement this book would have never come into being. Finally, to Veronica Kiley and Cindy Stone for their help with the manuscript, and to Daniel Stone, who has done such a magnificent job of the photography.

Library of Congress Catalog Card Number: 74–80304
Printed in the United States of America
Published simultaneously in Canada by General Publishing Company Limited

Design by Nedda Balter

Contents

Preface

My original intention in writing this book was to try to direct attention to the export ceramic wares Japan produced during the last hundred years, but—once started on this project—it seemed better to include all classes of Japanese ceramic wares of the period.

In my opinion the export wares produced since 1868 have been unjustly maligned in many cases, and the better pieces totally ignored. Although it is true that a lot of worthless junk was produced during this period, and even the best pieces do not measure up to the beauty and fineness of the old wares, there are many good pieces to be found.

The Japanese have long been an art-oriented society, with a deep love of and respect for nature, as illustrated by these quotations from two Japanese who lived twelve hundred years apart. Said the eighth-century Empress Komio, in a poem in which she speaks of offering flowers to the Buddha at Nara:

If I pluck them, the touch of my hand will defile; therefore standing in the meadows as they are I offer these wind-blown flowers to the Buddhas of the past, present, and the future. Translation by Okakura Kakuzō.

And Dr. Yanagi Sōetsu (1889–1961) said:

To me the greatest thing is to live beauty in our daily life and to crowd every moment with things of beauty.

Craftsmen practiced their skills from generation to generation, and whole areas produced a similar kind of art. Theirs is the true way of learning an art, absorbing it from all sides as children, observing their elders working in a centuries-old tradition, trial and error having been the great teacher. In this way art runs in the blood. It cannot be learned and assimilated in a few short years of schooling, as we so often vainly think.

In this last statement we also have the source of the Japanese disasters in their adventures with Western art styles. They could not learn and absorb teachings from the West in just a few years. It took us hundreds of years to evolve our styles, the good and the bad, and to learn to differentiate between the two.

In their enthusiasm for the new, the Japanese took everything Western and threw it back at us in ways that they thought were pleasing to our taste; they did not like the results and neither did we. However, when the Japanese took our methods and used them to please themselves, then they produced works of art in a new style. Perhaps it was not always great art, but it was produced with an artist's individuality.

Osbert Sitwell described Japanese gardens as being the great works of little masters, and the description could be applied to so much that was produced by the Japanese. In this book I have tried to show the great works of the little masters, and to help others see the difference between the good and the bad.

The Japanese approach to ceramics is artistic. Each part is allowed to develop its own character and grow together to form a pleasing whole, which no more needs to be perfect than does anything else in nature. The clays become what they are; if they are gray and coarse, so they will develop and be used as they are—to their best advantage. Nothing will be made to masquerade as what it is not.

The Japanese do not prize whiteness and translucency in porcelain as we do in the West, and, of course, an off-white or gray sets off the enamel colors far more kindly than does a brilliant white. In any case the Japanese prefer pottery to porcelain, and this preference has been influenced by the interior of their homes. Pottery with its softer appearance is much more compatible with the natural woods used in their houses. Herein, too, lies the explanation for the difference in coloring between Japanese and Chinese wares. The Chinese favor dark polished woods, and the colors they use on their ceramics are those that look well against such a background. In the West we lay a dazzling white cloth on the table for formal dining, and our tablewares must show to their best advantage in this setting. White porcelain and bright enamels sparkle in the light and gleam compatibly with the shining silverware. But as we slip away from formality these days, pottery with its quieter tones seems more in keeping with the times—so, fashions and tastes change.

The snob often pretends to good taste, being terrified of being accused of having bad taste or of being old-fashioned. In actual fact to have so-called good taste one must admire the fashions of the moment, and, of course, fashions change from year to year. This stems from two main causes—because manufacturers want to sell their wares and because conditions, economic and otherwise, constantly change. That which is good, however, will survive. Good art will always survive; it may be pushed aside for a time, but it will be there to return again.

The Japanese have changed their feelings for Western things several times. After the opening of Japan in the second half of the nineteenth century there was a great surge of feeling for all things Western. Their own things were forgotten for a time, but in the early part of this century their taste swung back again, and although they produced mountains of cheap goods for the foreign market, they wished for none of it for themselves. It was during this era that the words "Made in Japan" became practically synonymous with "junk."

The more one thinks about it, the more extraordinary it seems that a country which could produce articles of such exquisite workmanship, a country where craftsmen could take such infinite pains over details, would produce such cheap, shoddy stuff for the foreign market.

After World War II, during the Occupation, once again Western ways were held to be good, but now, twenty-five years later, the pendulum has swung back again. As far as modern pottery is concerned, Japan is an acknowledged leader.

The better export wares of the post-1868 years are neglected mainly because they are not in the traditional style of Japanese wares, and although made in European style, not European either. When I first began to be interested in them I found that practically no information was available. What distressed me even more was that people who held European porcelain in high regard would pass up a similar piece if they knew it was made for export in post-1868 Japan. As so many of the Japanese porcelains were made far more artistically than the corresponding European pieces, this seemed rather unfortunate. Consequently, I determined to search out what information I could find, and write a book to help other people evaluate these wares and form their own judgments.

As far as my brief survey of older wares is concerned, I have tried to steer a middle course as to dates and other controversial matters. I do not pretend to be an authority on those wares, but as this book is directed primarily at the less advanced collector, I wished to provide a brief historical background of Japan and her tradition of ceramics. For this reason the illustrations in this book are exclusively of pieces either in the United States or in England, so that readers can go and see these wares. Pictures of famous pieces in Japan can be seen in other books.

I have made particular mention of the two Morse collections of Japanese pottery, one in the Museum of Fine Arts, Boston, and the other at the Peabody Museum, Salem, Massachusetts, as it seems a pity that they are not more widely known and visited. Although the pieces in the collections may not be of such fine quality as those in Japan, at least they are available in this country. In London there is a collection of the same period at the Victoria and Albert Museum; it consists of the wares sent from Japan to the Centennial Exposition in Philadelphia in 1876.

On a recent visit to England I realized that a book about Japanese ceramics exported to the United States would also be of great help to British collectors. The import regulations were far more stringent here than in England, and this resulted in more precise markings, which changed from time to time. These markings are a great help when it comes to giving approximate dates for pieces, dates being one of the many problems with Japanese ceramics. The post-1868 export pieces I have seen in England were either unmarked or had Japanese characters inscribed on them (these inscriptions generally give no useful information), so if British collectors can compare their pieces with those in the United States, they will be at least a little better off.

Throughout the book I have used the Japanese order for names—the family name first, then the given or art name afterward. Japanese potters were always known by their art names, and generally are still so known today in Japan. However, present-day potters are usually known abroad by their family names, except in the few cases when they have succeeded to a renowned family art name.

The spelling of Japanese names is another problem, and again I have tried to steer a middle course. Vowels are pronounced much as in Italian, and if one follows another, each is pronounced separately. For example, Kakiemon: Kaki-yemon. The line over a vowel (ō or ū) gives it a long sound.

Certain of the better known symbols stamped on the backs of export wares are included in an appendix at the end of the book. As explained in Chapter 15, these backstamps have little bearing on the relative quality of the wares, and so a complete list has not been attempted.

Introduction

1

Japan and Her Ceramic Wares before 1868

Japan is a beautiful country with rugged coastlines, mountains, lakes, and forests, with an infinite variety of color in its spectacular sunsets, mists, and rain. It is also a poor country, with no gemstones and very little gold or marble. Because of the lack of such resources, perhaps, the art of Japan closely imitates nature, and her craftsmen display a heightened sense of color and balance in their work.

To the Japanese art is an integral part of life, and the potter has always been considered an artist with no distinction being made between the "fine" arts, the "industrial" arts, or the "decorative" arts. Japan may be a poor country from the point of view of its natural resources, but it is a country of untold wealth as far as its art is concerned. In the art of a country lies a concrete record of its past. The ceramic art of a country in particular provides a most comprehensive record, for it covers the tastes and needs of all the people, rich and poor alike. We can touch these things and begin to understand the people of a bygone age and how they lived.

Jōmon Period: The neolithic age in Japan is called the Jōmon Period, the name being derived from the pottery made during this time. "Jōmon" means rope pattern; the decorations were made by winding ropes around the body of the vessels (Ill. 1). It is interesting that the name of this early period

1. Jōmon urn, c. 2000 B.C. H. 15½". D. 13". These terra-cotta wares were fired at a relatively low temperature. "Urn" is the correct term for a large vessel of this nature, but on account of its association with funerary wares it can be misleading when used for wares of an early period. The Jōmon vessels were essentially for use by living people for cooking and storage purposes. The tapered base enabled the vessel to be placed in a hole in the ground, which was early man's method of keeping his pots steady on an irregular surface. Cleveland Museum of Art, Purchase, John L. Severance Fund

2. *Jōmon vessel, late Jōmon Period.* Private Collection

should come from the type of pottery used, in contrast to the term Stone Age in Europe, which is derived from the primitive tools and weapons used there in that period.

The Jōmon culture was based on a hunting and fishing economy, and, although it extended throughout the whole land, most of the Jōmon remains have been found in eastern Japan. Jōmon pottery is a dull gray, the vessels being made by the coil method. Mainly these vessels were used for boiling game and fish; many were of the type that tapered almost to a point at the bottom so that they could be sunk into the ground in the embers of the fire. It is generally accepted that the earliest Jōmon wares were made about 5000 B.C. and that the period extended to about 200 B.C., when the Yayoi Period began.

Yayoi Period: The Yayoi culture came from Korea and spread from the western part of Japan, bringing agriculture with it. A little kingdom and government were established on the Yamato plains. The emperors of Japan are direct descendants of the Yamato kings, who were priests as well as rulers. The imperial line claimed descent from the Sun Goddess and, among other things, this later gave the emperors a suitably impressive background for communications with China. The three symbols of imperial authority—they are still so today—came to Japan by way of Korea: a semiprecious stone curved like a huge comma, which is a common archaeological find in Korea; the

iron sword from continental Asia; and the bronze mirror, which is a symbol of the sun, from China. Seen from a Western point of view, these three items seem at first to form a somewhat bizarre collection for an imperial regalia. However, as Japan was still in the Stone Age when they were introduced into that country, the iron sword and bronze mirror must have seemed truly wondrous objects to the Japanese and deserving to become imperial possessions.

Pottery of the Yayoi Period (200 B.C.–A.D. 250) was of a warm russet color, and with the emergence of the rice-based economy, storage jars were needed. Bottles, pitchers, and footed jars were common forms. Both Jōmon and Yayoi pottery were low-fired wares. No remains of special kilns for firing pottery from these periods have been found.

Kofun Period: The Kofun, or Grave Mound, Period (A.D. 250–552) saw the development of Hajiki wares, which were very similar to Yayoi wares, but shaping techniques had advanced and new forms appeared. Haniwa figures were made to be placed around royal tombs. Up to this time, as in China, when an emperor or prince died most of his attendants and followers were buried alive with him, a rather distressing custom. However, according to tradition, the Emperor Suinin changed this practice, and clay figures of people and animals standing on circular bases were substituted for the real thing (Ills. 3 and 4). Descendants of the

3. *Haniwa horse. H. 23½". L. 26". Kofun Period* A.D. *250–552. Royal tombs were encircled with terracotta figures of all kinds—warriors, ladies, animals, birds, models of houses, and so on. They were originally made as substitutes for live members of the royal entourage.* Cleveland Museum of Art, Norweb Collection

4. *Haniwa head, female, showing headdress. 5th–7th century* A.D. Metropolitan Museum of Art, New York, Rogers Fund

haniwa makers, who settled at Toki-mura, near Osaka, are still making pottery there to this day.

Around A.D. 400 Sueki pottery, or Sue ware, a high-grade stoneware, made its appearance. It was a gray brown color, and because of the new methods of firing, was very hard and strong. The technique for making this type of ware came to Japan from Korea. Special sloping kilns were constructed for the purpose—either a tunnel built into a hillside or a ditch roofed over. They could achieve a temperature of about 1825° F. The potter's wheel was also introduced during this period.

With these new methods the type of clay employed was of great importance: It had to be able to withstand the high temperatures without melting into a puddle. The increased heat was responsible for another new development—the natural glaze. When ashes from the fire fell on the wares in the

5. *Terra-cotta jar. Sue ware, Kofun Period, c. A.D. 500. Thickly potted in a rare shape, this piece has a natural glaze resulting from the high temperature in the kiln. There are several small jars on the shoulder, although unfortunately some are fragmentary.* Courtesy of the Brooklyn Museum, Gift of Mrs. Albert H. Clayburgh

kiln, a natural glaze resulted; this might vary from green to brown (Ill. 5).

Asuka Period: Although the *sueki* wares were the products of a superior technique, *hajiki* wares still continued to be made throughout the Asuka Period (A.D. 552–646). It is a characteristic of Japanese ceramics that a new style does not necessarily supersede an older one; the older style continues to be produced side by side with the new. However, *hajiki* wares clung to the traditional style, and were used by the ordinary people; *sueki* wares, with their foreign background, found favor with the court and aristocracy (Ill. 6).

Through the ages Japan has undergone periods of great influence from other lands, when she has taken as much as she wished from other countries and civilizations she admires, then has retreated to the fastness of her islands, absorbed what she has learned, and adapted it to suit her own character and needs. From A.D. 600 to 800, for example, Japan learned as much as she could from China. Students and scholars were sent there, and Buddhist missionaries went from China to Japan. As well as Buddhism, the Chinese written language was brought to Japan, as was Chinese money.

6. *Arc-shaped tile. Asuka Period (A.D. 552–646). Made of light gray clay, it was probably whitewashed on the outer surface. Tiles of this type were used under the eaves.* Courtesy of the Brooklyn Museum, Carll H. De Silver Fund and Others

Buddhism was originally an Indian religion. It traveled by way of China and Korea to Japan, where it was adapted to fit in with their own native Shinto religion, a simple nature worship—each aspect of nature was believed to have its own god: the sun, wind, rocks, trees, flowers, and so on. Shrines were built in beautiful and awe-inspiring places, and the Torii, or gate, purified the visitor. Buddhist deities were accepted as being the same as the Shinto ones, under different names, and as Buddhism was an ethical religion and Shinto a nature worship, there was no conflict between the two.

Appreciation of nature has always played a great part in Japanese life, particularly the principle that in nature there is balance but not symmetry. Simplicity and understatement are other principles generally basic to all their art. Given a choice, they prefer to be obscure rather than over-explicit.

By the eighth century Chinese civilization was declining; the last official Japanese mission was sent there in 838. The Japanese adapted what they had learned from the Chinese to fit their own needs. Nara, the first Japanese capital, laid out in 710, was copied from the Chinese capital of Ch'ang-an.

During the Nara Period (646–794) both the *hajiki* and *sueki* styles of pottery continued to flourish (Ill. 7), and, in addition, a new kind of pottery appeared. This was Nara *sansai*, or "three color." These wares are softly curved and have dappled glazes of greens and browns on a white ground (Ill.8). They were the first Japanese wares to be deliberately glazed, and they were made in a great variety of forms. Cups, jars, bowls, dishes, vases, and incense burners were decorated either with the three colors or else with a green glaze patterned with green spots.

The court did not stay long at Nara, but moved to Kyoto in 794. Kyoto, which means "capital," is about thirty miles north of Nara. It also was laid out like Ch'ang-an. At that time it was called Heian, meaning "peace and tranquillity."

The Heian age is looked on as a kind of Utopian age. Literature, art, and handicrafts flourished; magnificent temples, pagodas, and monasteries were built around the city. The Chinese system of administration and taxation, adopted by the Japanese, provided great wealth for the nobles and extreme poverty and toil for the peasants. In China government was by men of ability; in Japan

7. Jar. Sue ware, Nara Period (646–794). Natural glaze has run onto the shoulder. The shape of the piece appears to have been inspired by a piece of Chinese bronze. Private Collection

8. Jar. Nara sansai *(three-color glaze). Eighth century.* Private Collection

9. *Large grain storage jar. Stoneware, Shigaraki ware, fourteenth century. Shigaraki is one of the Six Ancient Kilns. The local clay is heavy, coarse, and full of fine quartz particles, which come to the surface when the pot is fired. This piece, which is a particularly fine one, has a natural ash glaze with amber-colored scorch marks.* Courtesy of the Brooklyn Museum, Frank L. Babbott Fund

administrative posts became hereditary, and consequently the administration deteriorated. Men were more interested in the niceties of life, as long as the money came from somewhere.

The Heian age was the great age of poetry—every refined person was expected to be able to write a poem at any given moment about anything. This requirement was one of the great dividing lines between the courtiers and the rising class of knights in the provinces; the knights were fighting men on horseback, not poets. The court ladies were the novelists. These ladies had an incredible amount of spare time on their hands—they sat around in the half dark, hardly seeing anyone. Their main preoccupation was what to do with their leisure time, and what some of them did was to write novels and diaries. The men learned to speak and write Chinese, and the Chinese language carried great prestige, but the ladies did not learn it. They wrote their novels in Japanese.

Green glazed wares were still produced during the Heian Period (794–1185). Sueki wares underwent a change in the middle of the tenth century with the introduction of a new firing technique. Oxidizing flames

10. *Jar. Tamba ware. Muromachi Period (1333–1568). This piece is a dark red brown with a natural ash glaze.* Private Collection

could now be produced, and this resulted in bright off-white wares, instead of the coarse iron gray pottery produced by the reduction process.

These elegant and refined whiter wares, often decorated with a pale green transparent glaze, are called Heian *shiki*. Reflecting the aesthetic taste of the Heian aristocracy, they were made in a wide variety of forms: dishes, bowls, pouring vessels with attached handles, ink stones, and so on. As the Heian Period declined, the emperor no longer did the actual ruling; it was done by the Fujiwara family in the shadows behind the emperor. The military deteriorated into a kind of ceremonial color-guard.

Kamakura Period: The nonpoetic knights in the provinces gained more power and became virtually independent of any control from Kyoto. In the mid-twelfth century two factions, the Taira and the Minamoto, fought with each other, and when the Taira faction had been completely crushed, Yoritomo Minamoto had himself proclaimed shogun, or generalissimo. He became military dictator and settled in Kamakura, where the provincial warriors, the samurai, became the dominant class. The Kamakura Period (1185–1333) saw a great change in the most favored pottery style. The court aristocracy were no longer the prevailing arbiters of taste; now it was the turn of the provincial landowners and the military class. The new type of ware was a rough sort of *sueki* teabowl, the *yama-jawan*. The clay used was of a very course nature, and the bowls were turned on a wheel at high speed. The foot was often attached afterward by hand to save time.

This period also saw the development of the Six Ancient Kilns, with wares ranging from the thickly glazed utensils of old Seto to the unglazed strictly utilitarian wares of Bizen, Shigaraki, and Tamba (Ills. 9 and 10).

Muromachi Period: The Kamakura shogunate was overthrown in 1334 by the defecting general Ashikaga, who set up his own shogunate in Kyoto. This shogunate was not as strong as the Kamakura had been, and for two hundred years there were civil wars. Emperors reigned, shoguns ruled, and independent petty domains warred against each other. This was the age of the so-called Japanese pirates, who were not pirates in the modern sense of the word, but were owners of large fleets of boats that roamed the seas even as far away as Siam. Trading ships came and went from the fast-growing port of Osaka. This period is called the Muromachi Period (1333–1568), after the street in Kyoto where Ashikaga's palace stood.

Tea drinking had been popular with the aristocracy and the clergy since the thirteenth century, but during the Muromachi Period it spread to the provinces, where the samurai and other well-situated persons enjoyed it.

Murata Jukō, "father of the tea ceremony" (1423–1502), laid down the rules for it, and the tea master Takeno Jō-ō (1502–1555) helped spread the fashion of secular tea drinking. Middle-class citizens and merchants in the cities, as well as the smaller landowners in the provinces, took up the custom, and so the demand for suitable utensils increased.

The Six Ancient Kilns continued their production, but a new type of ware emerged in the Mino area. This was yellow Seto, a light-toned yellowware made from the fine white clay of that area.

By now Europeans were exploring the East, and in 1543 a Portuguese ship was wrecked off Japan. The strange-looking sailors were welcomed by the Japanese, who, among other things, were fascinated by their guns and learned to make some for themselves. When the Portuguese eventually returned home by way of Korea and China, where European trade was already established, they told about the strange new land. Soon Portugal sent trading ships, complete with missionaries, as missionaries were always part of these expeditions, and trading was begun. The missionaries made converts. Within a short time the Dutch and English also started to trade with Japan, but they were different in that they did not take missionaries along.

The end of the civil war period was

brought about by Oda Nobunaga, who was a powerful daimyo, or lord, in the provinces. After he had gained enough strength by conquering his neighbors, he invaded Kyoto in 1568 and overthrew the shogunate, but although he became undisputed ruler of central Japan, he never succeeded in unifying the whole country. This was known as the Momoyama Period.

Oda Nobunaga, a devotee of the tea ceremony, owned a large collection of tea utensils, a fact mentioned in a letter from the Jesuit father Luis Frois, who visited Japan in the sixteenth century.

When Nobunaga was assassinated in 1582, Toyotomi Hideyoshi, his ablest general, took charge. After building a strongly fortified castle at Osaka, he established his government there. The castle was enormous, with an outer courtyard eight miles in circumference; tens of thousands of workmen were employed in its construction.

Hideyoshi was a man of humble birth, the only one of such origin to achieve greatness in those times. Doubtless this accounted for his love of lavish display and splendor. He was also a very small man, scarcely five feet tall, with a face said to resemble that of a wizened ape.

The name of this period, Momoyama, or "Peach Hill" (1568–1615), is derived from the site of a new fortified palace Hideyoshi built in 1594 on a hill on the southern edge of Kyoto. The palace was dismantled after Hideyoshi's death, and about a century later the whole hillside site was planted with peach trees. Hideyoshi managed to unify Japan within eight years. He decreed that all missionaries must leave because he was afraid they would be followed by soldiers, as had happened in other countries. By this time tea drinking had become a firmly established custom among the whole population, and Hideyoshi, an inveterate tea drinker, ordered the tea master Sen-no-Rikyū to revise and put into writing the rules of the tea ceremony. Rikyū favored a simple and rather monasterial concept of the ceremony. The first independent tearoom, built apart from the house, was his creation. This room was similar to a simple fisherman's hut, with a door so low that guests must enter it kneeling (Ill. 11). The tea ceremony was of such importance to Hideyoshi and his officers that they took teabowls and tea jars on campaign so that they could drink tea on the battlefield. Tea masters even accompanied the military on their campaigns.

Hideyoshi was famous for his huge tea parties, the most well known of which was held in 1587 at the Kitano pine grove near Kyoto. Everyone was invited—all the tea

11. Interior of the Tea House Ceremonial Room at the Philadelphia Museum of Art. Philadelphia Museum of Art; Photograph by A. J. Wyatt

masters of Japan and all the people regardless of class or social distinctions. More than 550 tea masters attended, bringing all their treasures and displaying their art and famous utensils for the admiration of the huge crowds. Hideyoshi conducted his own tea ceremony for a few chosen guests, then went to taste the tea made by the various masters. One hopes that he only had a small sip of each; otherwise he must have drunk an incredible amount of tea. Unfortunately, a rebellion broke out in Higo. Hideyoshi had to leave immediately to quell it, thereby breaking up the great tea party, which had to be terminated after only one day instead of lasting the planned ten days. But the spectacular affair has remained a historical highlight to this day.

Hideyoshi died in 1598 and Tokugawa Ieyasu became shogun in 1603, the same year

Christianity was suppressed, although it was not finally crushed until 1637. This action was not taken because of its religious point of view, but because Christians held a vague kind of allegiance to a foreign pope, which was not desirable.

Trade with Portugal was also stopped, but the Dutch were allowed to use one port, Nagasaki. Their merchants lived on an island in the bay, virtually imprisoned, and could not go to the mainland. No Japanese living abroad could return to Japan, and if he did he was executed; and no Japanese could go abroad. Only small ships were allowed to be built, those that could go no farther than between the four main islands. And any foreigner arriving in Japan, shipwrecked or otherwise, was to be executed.

Japan was now a closed country—peaceful, unified—and so it remained for

12. *Bowl, Seto ware, seventeenth century. The decoration is a Christian cross.* Philadelphia Museum of Art, John T. Morris Fund; Photograph by A. J. Wyatt

that Queen Elizabeth I of England died. Ieyasu established his capital at Edo, which was only a small village at the time. Edo became Tokyo in modern times.

Ieyasu built up a stable society and an efficient government. The people were divided into four rigid classes of society: the samurai, who could hold office and carry swords; farmers, who were rice growers and therefore essential to the well-being of the population; artisans, who produced goods; and finally, merchants and tradesmen, who formed the lowest class, being nonproductive.

two hundred years. Even the population did not increase.

During the Momoyama Period several new kinds of wares were made in the Seto-Mino area. White Shino wares, named for the tea master Shino Sōshin, who died in the early sixteenth century, are covered with a thick white feldspathic glaze; they were popular with contemporary persons of consequence (Ill. 13). The yellow Seto wares made in the Momoyama Period were of a deeper yellow than those produced in the Muromachi Period. Black Seto made its appearance at this time, the color being a much

13. *Stoneware dish, Shino ware; Momoyama or early Edo Period—late sixteenth or early seventeenth century. This is gray Shino, or* nezumi *(mouse gray) Shino. The leaf pattern is dark gray on a light gray ground.* Courtesy of the Brooklyn Museum, Gift of the Mary Griggs Burke Foundation

richer and purer black than anything yet made. Oribe wares, with their rich green glaze and new shapes, were the next type of ware to appear in the Mino area.

Furuta Oribe (1544–1615) was a tea master who served under all three lords—Nobunaga, Hideyoshi, and Ieyasu. He had been a pupil of Sen-no-Rikyū. His taste in tea ceremony wares has exerted a tremendous influence on Japanese ceramics down to the present time. The shapes he preferred were a complete break with the traditional styles, many pieces being in free-form designs.

Oribe became the tea teacher of Hidetada, son of Ieyasu, who succeeded his father as shogun . During the battle between Hidetada and Hideyori, Oribe visited different leaders to perform the tea ceremony for them. One day he needed a piece of bamboo to make a teaspoon, and while he was absorbed in his search for a suitable piece in the bamboo barricades, he was seen by the enemy and wounded, but fortunately was not killed.

14. *Sake bottle, Karatsu ware, seventeenth century. Karatsu wares bear a strong resemblance to Korean wares of the Yi Dynasty, which is not surprising as Korean potters made the Karatsu wares. Pieces with underglaze iron decoration, such as this one, are known as* E-garatsu, *or decorated Karatsu.* Philadelphia Museum of Art, given by S. E. Vanderslice; Photograph by A. J. Wyatt

Kobori Enshū (1579–1674) succeeded Oribe as tea master under the Tokugawa, and did much to encourage the production of tea ceremony wares.

Korean potters were brought to Japan at this time, and they settled in Kyushu and on the western tip of Honshu. Notable among the places where they settled are Karatsu and Satsuma, where they began to produce wares in Korean style (Ill. 14).

In the middle of the Momoyama Period an entirely new type of ware appeared in Kyoto. This was Raku, a light-bodied soft ware molded entirely by hand, and eminently suitable for the tea ceremony. Kyoto itself had no ceramic tradition, and these wares were first made by Chōjirō, a tile maker. Raku ware and tiles are baked in the same type of low temperature kiln and the bodies of both are similar.

Edo Period: With the opening of the Edo Period (1615–1868) came the discovery in 1616 of porcelain clay near Arita, in the province of Hizen, by Ri Sampei, a Korean potter. Some blue and white porcelain had already been made in Japan by Gorodaiyu Shonsui, who had visited China at the beginning of the sixteenth century and had worked for five years in the Ching-tê-Chên factories. When he returned to Japan he took a supply of the necessary materials with him, and made porcelain wares until his material ran out.

After the discovery of suitable local clays for porcelain making, kilns in the Arita area gradually turned from producing Korean-type wares as made at Karatsu to finer porcelain. These new wares were very popular, as the porcelain was much harder and more durable than pottery, and the white background showed off to advantage the underglaze blue decoration.

These blue and white wares were produced exclusively for about thirty years, and then an Imari ceramic dealer named Tojima Tokuzaemon learned the technique of overglaze enameling from a Chinese potter at Nagasaki. Tokuzaemon passed on the secret to Kakiemon, and after the two had worked and experimented together for a time, Kakiemon succeeded in applying overglaze enamels to his porcelain wares. This was around 1644 (the various sources do not agree on the exact date). Kakiemon decorated his wares sparingly, with rarely more than a third of the surface covered, so that the brilliant enamels enhanced and contrasted with the sparkling cream-colored glaze (Ill. 15). In time, the secret of enameling spread, and polychrome enamel porcelain wares were soon being produced by other Arita potters.

The first Japanese ceramics in Europe were probably taken there by the Portuguese at the end of the sixteenth century. By the mid-seventeenth century there was a flourishing export trade in Arita porcelains, which were sent to Europe by way of the Dutch colony at Nagasaki.

Chinese porcelains had been imported into Europe in large quantities, but because of the internal struggles in China the source

15. Bowl, Kakiemon ware, Arita Province. Early eighteenth century. This fine white porcelain bowl has overglaze enamel decoration in green, red, and blue. Courtesy of the Brooklyn Museum, Gift of Carll H. De Silver

16. A. *Imari dish, porcelain, eighteenth century. Decorated with overglaze enamels, with the character* JU, *symbol of longevity, in the center.* B. *Dish turned over to show details of the overglaze enamel decoration on the underside.* Courtesy, Museum of Fine Arts, Boston

had dried up and the Dutch East India Company jumped in to fill the void with the new Japanese porcelains from Arita. Blue and white ware in the Chinese tradition was shipped to Amsterdam, where the Dutch ceramists at Delft began to imitate it, since it was very popular and brought high prices.

Meanwhile, the Japanese began to make pieces especially for the European market, in European style, as described to them by the Dutch traders at Nagasaki. These were called Imari ware because they were exported from that port, although they were actually made in Arita (Ill. 16). These pieces, too, were in great demand, with the result

that during the eighteenth century many leading European factories began making pieces in the same style. The imitations were so well done that it is often hard to tell if a piece was made in Japan or not.

Kilns in other areas in Japan began to produce porcelain, notably the Nabeshima, Hirado, and Kutani kilns (Ill. 17).

Almost at the same time as Kakiemon discovered the secret of enameling porcelain, Ninsei in Kyoto succeeded in enameling his pottery wares. Ninsei was an extraordinarily skillful potter, and his tea jars are held in particularly high regard (Ill. 18). They were formed on the wheel with an impeccable technique, and each had its own pictorial design covering most of the surface.

Ogata Kenzan (1663–1743), a pupil of Ninsei, and brother of Kōrin, the celebrated painter, made pottery wares with simple enamel decoration in a free and bold style. The Kenzan line ofpotters continues down to this day, making wares in their traditional style.

Other Kyoto potters followed Ninsei and Kenzan, notably Eisen, Mokubei, Dōhachi, and Hozen, all master potters who produced highly original wares.

Besides all this progress, the old styles of wares were still being produced in much the same way as they had always been made, as, for example, at Tamba.

With the Meiji Period (1868–1912) came commercialism and the eclipse of the artist-craftsman.

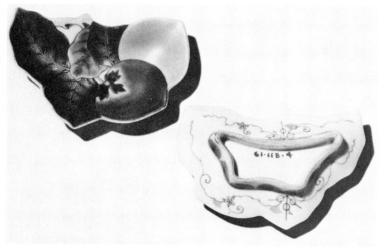

17. *Porcelain sauce dishes with overglaze enamel decoration. L. 4". H. ¾". Nabeshima ware, Genroku Period, c. 1680–1720.* Philadelphia Museum of Art, given by Mrs. Herbert C. Morris; Photograph by A. J. Wyatt

18. *Teabowl by Ninsei (mid-seventeenth century). Pottery with overglaze enamels in blue, red, and green, outlined in gold. This piece bears a strong resemblance to lacquer ware.* Metropolitan Museum of Art, Gift of Charles Stewart Smith

2

Tea, Tea Masters, and the Tea Ceremony

Tea

The tea ceremony has probably had more influence on Japanese taste than any other single factor in Japanese civilization. Besides creating the need for suitable wares for the ceremony itself, it has influenced all forms of Japanese art, as well as the costume, manners, and taste of all classes of Japanese. It has been variously described as an exercise in style in which the host seeks to create the most beautiful effects from the simplest possible means, or the art of concealing beauty that it may be discovered, or suggesting what you dare not reveal. Because of the simplicity and lack of ostentation of the tea ceremony, a poor man can put on as fine a one as a rich man.

Tea was first a medicine before it was a beverage. The plant is a native of southern China, and the early Chinese drank tea to relieve fatigue and to help their eyesight. They also made it into a paste and applied it externally for rheumatic pains. The Taoists believed that drinking tea was essential to the achievement of immortality. By the fourth and fifth centuries tea had become the favorite beverage of the inhabitants of the Yangtse-Kiang valley. They used it in cake form, the leaves being steamed, crushed, and made into a cake, which was then boiled with rice, ginger, orange peel, salt, spices, and milk. A remnant of this an-

cient method remains today in the Russian practice of using lemon slices in tea. The modern Chinese ideograph "cha" for tea was coined at about this time, and in England the slang expression for tea is still "char."

In the eighth century Luwuh, the Chinese poet, formulated the Code of Tea in his *Chaking*, a work consisting of ten chapters divided into three volumes. It described the nature of the tea plant, the implements for gathering the leaves, and the selection of the leaves; the necessary tea-making utensils, the desirable methods of making cake tea, and the vulgarity of the ordinary methods in use; a historical summary of illustrious tea drinkers, famous Chinese tea plantations, and possible variations of the tea service, with illustrations of the tea utensils. The final chapter is lost. Although cake tea was still in use, Luwuh eliminated all the other ingredients except salt.

During the Sung Dynasty (960–1280) whipped tea came into fashion. The leaves were ground to a fine powder, and the beverage was made by whipping the powder in hot water with a bamboo whisk; no salt was added. The Zen Buddhist monks originated a ritual that consisted of a formal gathering in front of a statue of the Bodhi-Dharma, where tea was drunk in solemnity from a single bowl.

After the Mongol invasions and the subsequent internal struggles in China, powdered tea was no longer used and finally became altogether forgotten. In the Ming Dynasty tea was made by steeping the leaves in hot water. Tea drinking was introduced into Europe at this time from China, the Europeans learning to make their tea by steeping it.

Tea was first introduced into Japan during the eighth century. It is recorded that in 729 the Emperor Shomu gave tea to one hundred monks at his palace in Nara, and Okakura says in *The Book of Tea* that the leaves were probably imported by Japanese ambassadors to the Tang court in China, and were prepared in the way then in fashion, which would be in the way described by Luwuh. In 801 the monk Saicho brought some seeds from China, which he planted in Yeisan. Cake tea was made from the tea leaves.

The Sung practice of grinding the leaves reached Japan in 1191, along with the tea ritual using the powdered whipped tea. By the thirteenth century the tea ceremony practiced by the Buddhist monks had spread throughout Japan, and in the next two hundred years it became an independent secular performance.

Tea Masters

The patronage of the Shogun Ashikaga Yoshimasa was largely responsible for the general adoption of the ceremony, but the tea masters were also influential. These tea masters were not potters themselves, but through their understanding of the aesthetics of tea and their perception of the simple beauty of unpretentious utensils, they set the standards of the tea ceremony and, as a direct result, of aristocratic taste. The utensils they preferred were simple everyday vessels that originally were not made for the ceremony at all—Korean rice bowls, for instance. The Japanese call such simple objects *shibui*—literally translated, "tastefully astringent."

The beauty that the tea masters discovered is often not readily apparent to the uninitiated, but they took great pride in their sensitivity to this kind of beauty. One day the tea master Kobori Enshū (1579–1647)

was being complimented by his disciples on the taste he had displayed in the choice of his collection. "Each piece is such that no one can help admiring it," they told him. "It shows that you had better taste than had Rikyū, for his collection could only be appreciated by one beholder in a thousand." Enshū replied, "This merely proves how commonplace I am. The great Rikyū dared to love only those objects which personally appealed to him, whereas I unconsciously cater to the taste of the majority. Verily, Rikyū was one in a thousand among tea masters."

It was Murata Jukō, a priest, who introduced the tea ceremony to the Shogun Ashikaga Yoshimasa. Jukō formalized the rules for the ritual, which became popular with the aristocracy. He was the friend of all the aesthetes of his day. One of his contemporaries, Sō-ami, or Nōami (1397–1471), became a famous tea master and is credited with being among the first to create a demand for suitable wares for the tea ceremony. Sō-ami was also a famous gardener and landscape painter in ink monochrome. During the next century, under the influence of the tea master Takeno Jō-ō, a skillful verse writer, the tea ceremony spread to the cities and city merchants began the practice of formal tea drinking.

All these tea masters created and shaped the basic forms of the tea ceremony—the gathering together of a few friends, the ritual of preparing and drinking the tea, eating the frugal meal, the type of utensils to be used, and so on. However, it was Sen-no-Rikyū (1521–1591) who introduced the concept of the small separate tearoom (Ill. 19).

Sen-no-Rikyū was the son of Tanaka Yohei, a wholesale fish dealer. He took the name Sen from his grandfather, an artist and friend of the Shogun Ashikaga Yoshimasa. The name Rikyū, given him by his Zen teacher, was confirmed by Imperial edict. He enjoyed the friendship of the Shogun Hideyoshi, who ordered him to revise and put into writing the rules of the tea ceremony. These rules covered every aspect of the ceremony: the ideal dimensions of the tearoom, the number of guests, the preparation of the tea, the selection of the food and

19. *Ceremonial Tea House, waiting room, and garden at the Philadelphia Museum of Art. The guests assemble in the waiting room at the right, then pass through the garden by the "dewy path," or* roji, *to the tearoom at the left.* Philadelphia Museum of Art; Photograph by A. J. Wyatt

the order in which the dishes should be presented, as well as the correct gestures of the host and guests.

At the age of seventy Rikyū was obliged to commit suicide on the order of his former friend, the Shogun Hideyoshi, who, some sources say, accused him of living in a style above his station in life. Others say that enemies of Rikyū told Hideyoshi that Rikyū was planning to administer a fatal dose of poison in a bowl of tea.

Two tea masters leave their names per-

petuated in special types of tea ceremony wares. They are Shino Sōshin and Furuta Oribe.

Shino Sōshin is associated with a type of pottery made at the Seto kilns (Ill. 20). Shino-*yaki* is still being made, wares with a thick soft cream-colored crackle glaze over designs sketchily drawn in iron pigment on the biscuit. Shino Sōshin is said to have originated incense guessing contests.

Furuta Oribe-no-Shō was born near Seto, the son of a former priest. He served

20. *Dish with design of three wild geese in flight.* Nezumi, or gray Shino ware, c. 1600. Cleveland Museum of Art, Mrs. A. Dean Perry Collection

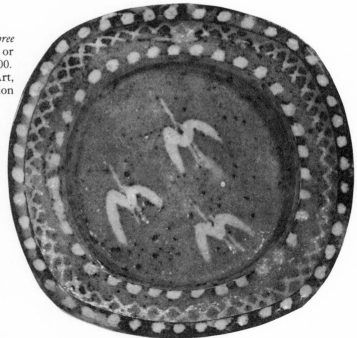

as samurai under Oda Nobunaga until the latter's death in 1582. In 1585 he was created a daimyo, lord, by Hideyoshi and put in charge of a castle near Kyoto, where he met Rikyū and became his pupil. Oribe was present at the famous tea party Hideyoshi held in 1585, which many great tea masters attended, but at that time he was little known.

After Hideyoshi's death Oribe had Ieyasu's son Hidetada as pupil. When Hidetada became the second Tokugawa shogun, Oribe's position as tea master was established, and daimyos competed to become his pupils. His taste became the predominant one of the period, and potters created wares to please his highly developed artistic sensibilities. Oribe had direct contact with foreign goods being imported in his time and these influenced his taste. He preferred wares in free-form shapes, which seem quite modernistic to our eyes; they are known as Oribe-*gonomi*, or Oribe-style wares.

Unfortunately, like Rikyū, Oribe was obliged to commit suicide at an advanced age. In 1614 a battle was fought between Hidetada, Oribe's pupil, and Hideyori, son of Oribe's former master and pupil, Hideyoshi. Oribe fought on the side of Hidetada. When the battle ended in a truce, a group of dissenters led by some of Oribe's retainers tried to set fire to the streets of Kyoto so that they could attack the Tokugawa forces, but this failed and the conspirators were discovered and taken prisoner. Oribe was held responsible for the acts of his retainers, although they had acted without his knowledge, and he had to commit *seppuku*, or hara-kiri. *Seppuku* is the term generally used in Japan; hara-kiri, although used by westerners, is considered a vulgar term in Japanese.

Kobori Enshū served under Ieyasu, and was a landscape designer, poet, painter, and calligraphist as well as tea master. He succeeded Oribe, but was a follower of the style of Sen-no-Rikyū, whose concept of the tea ceremony was monastic as opposed to the more social concept of Oribe. His name is associated with a type of pottery made at a number of kilns throughout Japan. These, known as Enshū's Seven Favorite Kilns, are Shidoro, Zeze, Kosobe, Agano, Takatori, Asahi, and Akahada. All of them, with the exception of Kosobe, are still in production today.

Tea Ceremony

The tea ceremony may be held at any time between 4:00 A.M. and 6:00 P.M., although evening tea is seldom held in the summer because of the mosquitoes, nor dawn tea in winter because of the cold.

The tea is made from green tea leaves ground to a fine powder, which is whipped in boiling water in the bowl with a handmade bamboo whisk to make a frothy jade green beverage. The foods must be a delight to behold, the colors harmonizing with the dishes in which they are served. A delicate fragrance of incense should pervade the room. The success of the tea ceremony lies in its simplicity and subtlety.

Sen-no-Rikyū modeled his tearoom, the *sukiya*, on the thatched huts of Buddhist recluses. He said that the room should not be larger than four and a half mats (8 square feet), and was to accommodate at the most five persons. The entrance should be small, like the entrance to a fisherman's hut. Rikyū's standard entrance was 23 by 27 inches, although a slightly larger entrance was permitted to allow the entry of Hideyoshi's generals wearing armor. The fittings of the room should be of the simplest, plaster and woodwork of the most ordinary kind; rare or precious things should not be used (Ill. 11). The room should suggest an atmosphere of refined poverty, with—ideally—only a simple wall scroll and flower arrangement in the *tokonama*, or alcove, as decoration. The utensils should be of the plainest, and the meal quite frugal, served by the host himself (Ill. 21).

Rikyū emphasized the simplicity of the ceremony, with no rich or out-of-season foods, and no bones or fins for the guests to crunch or spit out. The flowers should be of no more than two colors, arranged in a plain bamboo vase, with no smell to disturb the tranquillity. The scroll should preferably be the writing of a Zen priest or an old Japanese poet or, if a painting, be in ink with little or no color.

The garden through which the tearoom

21. Tray, Oribe ware. Private Collection

22. Kitchen of Ceremonial Tea House at the Philadelphia Museum of Art, showing utensils for the ceremony arranged on shelves. Philadelphia Museum of Art; Photograph by A. J. Wyatt

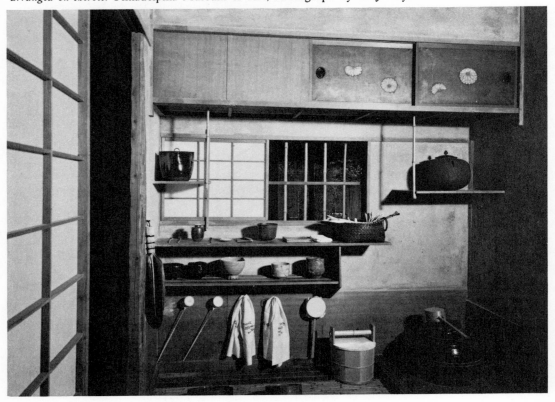

is approached is as important as the tearoom itself. Rikyū said that the path, or *roji*, should be of "thick green moss, all fair and sunny warm," suggesting a simple mountain path. Only common and naturally planted things are acceptable in the garden—evergreens are desirable, but flowers are out of place. The *roji* is intended to break connection with the outside world and prepare the guest for the full enjoyment of the aesthetic experience to come (Ill. 19).

The host makes his preparations for the tea on the day before the ceremony, getting up early to sweep and prepare the tearoom and garden. He puts fresh water, often from some special source, in the water basin, and arranges the flowers and utensils, which are to be of the simplest and roughest, but selected with great care to avoid any repetition. For instance, if the bowl has a black glaze, the tea caddy should not be of black lacquer.

Many utensils were given names that have since become famous; if the utensils were broken, they were mended with gold lacquer; broken ones that have been mended are highly desirable, and the decoration thus naturally formed is preferable to an elaborate decoration executed by the potter when

he made the piece. Such a piece is called a tribute piece, as no one would presume to make an unnoticeable repair, thereby passing off his own work as the master's. (See Ill. 23 for the teabowl by Kenzan, which not only has been repaired with long lacquer lines, but has a large triangular portion of gold lacquer showing on the front.) Teabowls vary according to season. A deep one is used in winter to conserve the heat, and a wide shallow one is used in summer. In Ill. 23 the teabowl by Kenzan is for summer, and the one by Raku Seisai is for winter.

On the day of the tea ceremony the host again rises early, perhaps at dawn if he wishes to pluck mushrooms and fresh herbs with the dew still on them, and select the fish at the fish market. He sees that all is in readiness in the tearoom and garden, and sprinkles water on the stepping-stones and spreads a few leaves in the garden to present a natural appearance.

The guests assemble in the *yoritsuke*, or waiting place, where there must be no talking or whispering (Ills. 24 and 25). The chief guest, selected in advance, acts as spokesman for the others. He leads the other guests through the garden to the tearoom, which he enters first. His place is near the

23. *Part of ceremonial tea set given by Okakura to Mrs. Jack Gardner of Boston.* Top left, *iron teakettle, early nineteenth century;* top right, *charcoal basket, mid-nineteenth century, and twig charcoal;* center, *pottery slop jar, Takatori ware, late nineteenth century;* bottom left, *pottery teabowl, "Cormorant Boat" by Kenzan (1663–1743), which has been extensively mended with gold lacquer;* bottom right, *pottery teabowl, "Black Peony" by Raku Seisai (early nineteenth century);* below, *two feather brushes, early twentieth century.* Isabella Stewart Gardner Museum, Boston

24. *Tea House waiting room, from the garden side.* Philadelphia Museum of Art; Photograph by A. J. Wyatt

tokonama, to the left of the host and facing him; he takes the lead at all times in the conversation, with intelligent questions and appropriate comments.

When the guests are seated on the floor the host brings in the necessary utensils with the exception of the brazier and kettle, which are already in place. According to a strict ritual, he prepares tea in the bowl for each guest in turn, who drinks the entire contents appreciatively, and returns the bowl to the host. The host then carefully wipes the bowl and prepares some for the next guest.

The meal, according to Rikyū, should be of the simplest, consisting of no more than two courses. The food served should be as appealing to the eye as to the taste, and, although simple in nature, requires considerable forethought on the part of the host. Tea diaries describing meals served by famous tea masters are still in existence; in one such diary the menu of a meal prepared by Jō-ō in 1554 is described and it included a bowl of minced sparrow broiled in bean paste. This is quite interesting, as sparrows were also eaten in England in Elizabethan times, but seem to have fallen out of favor since, except with cats.

After the meal the utensils are handed to the guests to be admired. Although the teabowls often seem crude and rough, they can cost as much as a hundred dollars. The guests then take their departure, refreshed by the aesthetic experience; the tea ceremony may take from forty minutes to four hours, depending on how elaborate it is.

At the present time there are at least twenty-four major schools of "tea" in Japan, the ceremony having become symbolic of a way of life. In fact, it has been described as being the flower of Japanese civilization.

25. *Tea House waiting room from the back, looking across the garden to the Ceremonial Tea House.* Philadelphia Museum of Art; Photograph by A. J. Wyatt

3

Traditional Japanese Ceramic Techniques

Ceramics are made from clay and baked in a kiln. The different kinds of ceramics, ranging from coarse earthenware to fine porcelain, depend on both the type of clay used and the heat and duration of the baking.

Ceramic clay has to have three properties: first, sufficient plasticity to be molded easily; second, the ability to hold its shape during firing; and third, a rocklike hardness after it has been fired at a suitable temperature. The main source of such clay is feldspar, which is the most common rock on this earth. Clay is weathered, or decomposed, feldspar, ground into particles, with the soluble elements removed. It falls into two categories: primary clay and secondary clay.

Primary, or residual, clay is found in the place where it was formed. It is a very pure clay, but its particles are rather coarse and uneven and it is relatively nonplastic. Secondary clay is formed when the rock is broken up by weathering and the pieces carried away by wind or running water, and finally deposited as silt to form a clay bed. This is the commonest type of clay. Its particles are uniform, fine-grained, and plastic, but contain many impurities.

The Chinese called the residual clay they found near Ching-tê-Chên "Kao-ling," which means "the high hills." Kaolin is a pure white clay but not plastic enough to be used alone, and it is difficult to fire satisfactorily. The Chinese also discovered petuntse (*pai-tun-tzū*), which is a less decomposed

feldspar that fuses into a kind of natural glass under heat. Together with the kaolin, water, and certain mineral salts, they found it made a pliable fine clay that fired at a high temperature to a pure white porcelain.

The Chinese called kaolin the "bones" and petuntse the "flesh." Père d'Entrecolles tells how the workers laughed when some Europeans stole petuntse briquettes and tried to make porcelain out of them. They said it was like trying to make a body without bones.

In Japan clays of all kinds have been used to make ceramics since very early times. Pottery has always been a craft practiced by a large segment of the population. Farmers in many areas, such as Tamba, spend hours every day making wares and tending their clay. Whole villages made pottery from local clays in this way as a secondary occupation.

The kind of clay used is one of the principal indications of where the piece was made. Arita clays are fine and white; Kutani clays are the roughest and very gray. Kyoto wares generally have a gray clay body, but this varies from potter to potter, as the local clays have long been used up and clays are now brought in and blended individually by each potter.

About three hundred years ago a form of semidecomposed feldspar was discovered in Kyushu that would make porcelain without the addition of anything else. This soft stone, called Amakusa stone, has to be well ground to make porcelain. Before its discovery as a potential porcelain clay, it had been used as a sword-sharpening stone. It is still used throughout Japan to make porcelain bodies.

Ceramics divide up roughly into the following categories, with various shades in between. Each category needs its own type of clay and length and temperature of firing.

Earthenware is usually made from natural clay and fired at a low temperature. It is nonvitreous—that is, it does not become transparent. It is usually dark in color, fairly soft and porous, and will not hold liquids unless glazed. Raku ware meets this description.

Faience is a French term loosely applied to glazed earthenware in general. Satsuma export wares are generally referred to as being faience.

Terra-cotta is made from natural clay, fired, and left unglazed. Jōmon, Yayoi, and Hajiki wares fall into ths category, as well as the *haniwa* figures. s terra-cotta wares are porous, they do r t make satisfactory vessels for holding liquids.

Stoneware can be mad either from certain natural clays or from prepared mixed clays. It is fired at a much higher temperature than earthenware, which is why not all natural clays are suitable for stoneware. The red clays in particular could not be fired at stoneware temperature—their melting point is too low, and they would simply melt. Stoneware is hard, vitreous, and able to hold water even when unglazed. The fired color ranges from a light gray to a darker gray or brown. Stoneware first appeared in Japan around A.D. 400, with the Sueki wares.

China is made from a mixture of kaolin, certain other clays, flint, and flux to lower the melting point. China undergoes two firings, the first at a very h temperature, after which the ware is to be in the biscuit stage, and the secon at a lower temperature for the glaze. China bodies are generally white. The term *china* is commonly used quite loosely to describe all tablewares and/or dishes.

Porcelain is fired at a still higher temperature than china. It is made from a mixture of kaolin and other clays, with the exception of the Amakusa stone mentioned above which can be used alone and makes such a

tough porcelain clay that it can even be turned on the wheel. Porcelain is made in one firing, in contrast to china, the body and glaze maturing together. It is the hardest and most vitreous of all ceramics. Porcelain is generally cast in molds. It has been made in Japan since 1616.

Glazes

Glaze is applied to most forms of ceramics. The early glazes were accidental, the result of wood ashes from the kiln fire falling on wares in the kiln and reacting chemically with the clay body.

A glaze produces a glasslike surface on ceramic wares. The glaze materials become vitreous, or glasslike, at a lower temperature than the ceramic body. The difference between a glaze and glass is that a glaze is a coating that becomes vitreous and fuses with the clay body during firing, whereas glass is melted first of all into a liquid and then made into objects. A glaze must not liquefy in the way that glass does or it would run off the ware during firing. Glazes are either produced directly by the action of heat on the body or they are applied before firing as a coating by painting, dipping, pouring, or spraying. Glazing compounds are many and varied.

Salt glazing is effected by throwing salt into the kiln when the temperature has reached its highest point; the vapors from the salt settle on the wares and produce a very hard glaze. The glaze on terra-cotta water pipes is produced by this method. In modern times Rosanjin has produced many fine pieces with salt glazing.

Lead sulfide, ground to a fine white powder and dusted or painted on the clay body, fuses with the surface to produce a smooth shiny glaze at a low temperature. This is a very old glaze. Raku wares have a lead and borax glaze.

Feldspar, when powdered and used alone, will give a milky glaze, and when limestone is added it will fuse at a lower temperature.

Ash glaze, composed of ashes, feldspar, and clay, requires a higher temperature, but is very durable.

Luster glaze is a modern commercial development in Japan. It consists of a thin metallic film on the basic glaze, either added directly to it for an overall effect or put on over a fired glaze surface in the same way as an overglaze enamel.

Crackle glaze has crazed and developed minute cracks. This effect can be created in more than one way. It can be caused by the composition of the glaze itself or it can be the result of a sudden cooling. Raku ware is taken straight from the hot kiln and put into cold water, the sudden shock causing the glaze to crack in all directions. As Raku is a soft porous ware, the cracks in the glaze allow water to penetrate the body, which thus is not waterproof. However, after much use the pores gradually close, and in the course of time the piece no longer leaves a damp mark where it has stood. Edward Morse, in his *Japanese Homes and Their Surroundings,* says that old tiles were considered far superior for roofing a house, and second-hand tiles were in great demand since they were waterproof because the pores had filled with dust and dirt. Raku ware and roofing tiles have much in common.

A crackle glaze can also be rendered waterproof by refiring the piece. Before it is returned to the kiln, underglaze color is rubbed into the crackle so that when the cracks close on the completion of the firing the crackle pattern will be visible in color. Satsuma ware made for export frequently has color rubbed into the crackle, but it is not generally returned to the kiln for sealing (Color Plate 4).

Various decorative effects can be obtained from using two or more glazes of different colors on the same piece. If several colors are added to the glaze, they create a beautiful effect where they run together.

Unless stilts are used in the kiln, the foot of the piece to be fired must be free from glaze or it will stick to the kiln shelf. On large pieces of porcelain a double foot is often found, the second one being a ring toward the center of the piece; this served as additional support during firing. Limoges and Nippon pieces both have the same double foot. Sometimes a bar or star at the center serves the same purpose.

Kilns and firing: The early Jōmon and Yayoi wares had been fired either in the open or in trenches, where the temperature did not rise above 1,350° or 1,475° F. Not until the Kofun Period were more efficient kilns constructed.

The *ana-gama,* or Korean-style cave kiln, was introduced about A.D. 400. The heat in these kilns could rise to as much as 2,200° or 2,375° F. As their name implies, these were semisubterranean kilns, constructed either by roofing over a ditch running up a hillside or by digging a tunnel parallel to the upward slope of the hill. The lower end was used as a firebox, and the smoke escaped out of the upper end. This type of wood-burning kiln is still used by individual studio potters.

In the sixteenth century the *nobori-gama,* or Korean climbing kiln, made its appearance. This type of kiln was really a series of *ana-gama* set one above the other on a hillside and connected to one another. The lowest chamber was fired first of all, and when the wares were done, that chamber was sealed; then the next one, which was already hot from the fire in the lower one, was fired. This process was continued all the way along the kiln, some kilns having as many as fifty chambers.

In the Meiji era European-style kilns and firing methods using coal, oil, or electricity were introduced. These are the commercial methods used today.

The first step after a piece is formed, whether by throwing, molding, pressing, or jiggering, is to let it dry out. In this process the piece shrinks, the fine-grained clays shrinking the most because they hold more water. The drying has to be carefully and evenly done or the piece will crack or warp. When all the water between the clay particles has evaporated, the piece is said to be in the leather-hard state; it is called greenware. The clay particles themselves will still be damp; the piece will not be truly dry until it is in the kiln with the temperature at the boiling point of water, 212° F.

The final drying in the kiln must take place quite slowly or the steam formed inside the pieces will cause them to burst. Footed pieces like the pre-Nippon vase (Color Plate 6) and the Satsuma *koro* (Ill. 162) have holes drilled in the hollow feet to allow the steam to escape without causing damage.

By the time the kiln temperature

reaches about 925° F., the piece has become dehydrated and an irreversible chemical change has taken place. The clay cannot be reclaimed and reused; it has lost its plasticity and it will not disintegrate in water. But it is now highly fragile.

The next state is reached when the temperature has risen to about 1,650° F. and the oxidation is complete, all the carbon having been burned up. When pieces are too close together in a kiln, carbon is trapped and appears on them as black marks. This is a feature of Raku ware. No doubt it was originally accidental when two pieces touched and a shadow appeared on the ware as a result, but such shadows subsequently were created purposely.

The next major change occurs when vitrification, or glassification, begins; the temperature has then passed the red-heat mark. At this temperature the clay begins to harden and tighten, and this causes some shrinkage. Some of the components melt into beads of glass, soak into the surrounding area, and act like glue. The higher the temperature and the better the quality of the clay, the harder and the more transparent it becomes. When a certain critical temperature is reached clay will melt into a kind of glass; therefore, the temperature has to be carefully regulated so that the clay achieves its rocklike quality but does not go into the melting stage. However, tea masters have always deeply appreciated certain wares that have become deformed in the firing, notably the crouching flower vases of Tamba ware.

Glazes, on the other hand, have to melt; that is why they are made up of substances that will melt at a lower temperature than the clay body.

Domestic Wares and Export Wares in Traditional Styles

Famous Old Kilns

Six Ancient Kilns: The term Six Ancient Kilns is the general name for the Seto, Echizen, Tokoname, Bizen, Tamba, and Shigaraki kilns, all of which have been making ceramic wares since very early days. Seto, Echizen, Tokoname, and Bizen all claim to go back to Heian days, descending from Sue kilns in those places. Tamba dates from the early Kamakura Period, and Shigaraki from the middle Muromachi Period, with a branch kiln established later at Iga.

The potters working at these kilns were farmers as well. They worked with a plentiful local supply of clay in a long tradition of craftsmanship, which had developed over the years; the pieces they produced were strictly utilitarian. It was this unpretentious quality that, among other things, was recognized and appreciated by the tea masters. With the natural glaze brought forth by the firing, and with no artificial decoration, such a piece is a natural aesthetic expression of the clay itself and the human labor needed to shape it. Wares from the different kilns bear a strong resemblance to one another, as both the local clays and the techniques used were similar.

Seto: The ancient village of Seto is situated in Owari Province, ten miles northeast of the modern town of Nagoya, the capital of the region. The old kilns stood in a horseshoe around the village, and there were many of them. They continued making pot-

26. *Large heavily potted dish, Seto ware, with "Horse Eye" design. This type of ware was intended for peasant use, and is made of heavy gray pottery, covered with pitted and crackled buff glaze. C. 1840.* Courtesy of the Brooklyn Museum

27. *Vase, Seto ware. H. 10". This piece is decorated with an incised* tomoe *design, and has a yellowish green wood-ash glaze. This, and some other vases like it, were originally thought to be from the Kamakura Period, but recently it was discovered that they are all modern pieces, made in Seto by members of the Kito family.* British Museum

tery down to recent times, when they were either shut down or turned over to making porcelain (Ill. 26). Today Seto is the largest industrial porcelain-making area in the whole world, kilns standing side by side throughout the area. By day the sky is black with their smoke; by night flames shoot upward through the darkness, and day and night the rivers run white from the clay.

Ko-Seto (old Seto) wares. Fine quality clay of great plasticity and of high fire resistance was found in large quantities in the neighborhood of Seto, and stonewares covered with a thick glaze were made from it. Large pieces, like huge water jugs and storage jars, were built by the coil method, but smaller pieces were thrown on the wheel. The wood ash glazes varied from amber to dark brown and yellowish green. Some pieces were decorated with incised designs of plants, Flower Seto, or arabesques, some with a simple stamped device, and others with a raised applied decoration.

There are similar pieces in existence with the designs more deeply incised and a darker green or yellow brown glaze. These for a long time were believed to have been made at about the same date as the Flower Seto, and many were considered in Japan to be pieces of national importance. It now appears, however, that the Japanese authorities were victims of a deception, as two members of the Kato family, both living in Seto, have owned up to making them. The British Museum vase (Ill. 27), according to Soame Jenyns, seems to belong to this family.

During the civil wars in the fifteenth and sixteenth centuries the area around Seto was devastated time after time, and in the mid-sixteenth century the potters moved from there to Mino. Here totally different styles came into being—Ki-Seto (yellow Seto), Setoguro (black Seto), as well as Shino and Oribe wares.

Ki-Seto (yellow Seto). These wares are usually small dishes, flat bowls, incense burners, or boxes. They are decorated with a yellow glaze splashed with green, often over simple incised designs of a plant or vegetable. It has been suggested that the potters were trying to produce glazed wares similar to the celadons of Sung China, but their kilns were inadequate for the purpose. Ki-Seto wares date from the end of the sixteenth century.

Setoguro, black Seto wares, are a small group, consisting mostly of teabowls. This was the first appearance in Japan of a rich true black glaze, called *temmoku* in Japanese.

Shino wares. These wares were made under the direction of the tea master Shino Sōshin, and are almost exclusively tea ceremony pieces. They are heavy, with thick walls and deep cracks in the body. The most important categories are the white or plain Shino, the decorated Shino, and the gray Shino. The white Shino pieces are covered with a thick white feldspathic glaze, the first

28. *Footed cake dish, E-Shino ware (decorated Shino). Early nineteenth century.* Philadelphia Museum of Art, given by Theodore T. Newbold; Photograph by A. J. Wyatt

Japanese ceramics to have a white glaze. The E-Shino, or painted Shino wares, have a few graceful brushstrokes of cobalt blue or iron brown, representing grasses or birds (Ill. 28). Nezumi Shino (mouse gray) was first covered with iron slip, through which the designs were scratched; then a thick feldspathic glaze was applied and the piece fired. The iron slip turned a warm gray and the designs appeared white (Ills. 13 and 20).

Oribe wares. These wares reflect the taste of Furuta Oribe. Instead of the tradi-

tional styles, Oribe wares adopted new shapes, sometimes using distortion and imbalance in artistic ways. Square deep dishes, fan-shaped dishes, and linked rectangular dishes are typical shapes, with very simple designs. However, there were also plates, bowls of all kinds, lidded vessels, sake bottles, water jars, incense burners, incense boxes, sweetmeat jars, and jars for powdered tea, as well as teabowls (Ill. 29).

Besides the wide variety of forms, there was also great variety in the decoration.

29. *Sweetmeat jar, Oribe ware. Momoyama Period, sixteenth–seventeenth century. This is a rare piece. It has a tan glaze with overglaze decoration of white slip and green and brownish black glazes.* Courtesy of the Brooklyn Museum, Gift of Robert B. Woodward

Fig. 1. Map showing the principal Japanese kilns.

1. Hongo
2. Mashiko
3. Edo (Tokyo) Banko
4. Echizen
5. Kutani
6. Mino
7. Seto
8. Tokoname
9. Iga
10. Shigaraki
11. Zeze
12. Kyoto
13. Kosobe
14. Asahi
15. Akahada
16. Awaji
17. Tamba
18. Bizen
19. Hagi
20. Agano
21. Takatori
22. Karatsu
23. Arita (Imari,
    Kakiemon, Nabeshima)
24. Hirado
25. Koishibara
26. Onda
27. Satsuma
    (Ryumonji,
    Naeshirogawa)

Green Oribe is covered with a copper green glaze, some pieces having underglaze designs in brown iron oxide. Narumi Oribe has green glazes on a white slip and black Oribe wares have black glazes instead of the usual green. There are many more varieties of Oribe wares.

Echizen: The Echizen kiln sites are located in the northwest part of Japan, not far from Kutani. They date from late Heian days, but most of the kilns had ceased production by the mid-sixteenth century. However, the Taira kiln has continued production down to the present day, and the potters working there are descendants of the old families.

The production of these kilns was small, mostly kitchen utensils, which included some huge water jars. These wares have a green natural ash glaze, which drips richly over a dark brown body.

Tokoname: Traces of more than three hundred Tokoname kiln sites have been discovered in an area about twenty miles south of Nagoya. Jars and vases produced by these kilns were much favored by the tea masters

of the Muromachi Period. The high-fired unglazed stonewares, which are similar to the Echizen wares, have a rich warm brown body with a natural green glaze on the upper portions.

The kilns fell into decline in the seventeenth century, although wares were still produced in small quantities. Pieces made during the Meiji era have a yellow glaze over a red brown body. Today bricks and tiles are produced at Tokoname.

Bizen: Bizen stoneware was made in the vicinity of Imbe, in the province of Bizen. The *ko*-Bizen (old Bizen) wares are also known as Imbe-*yaki* (Imbe wares).

During the early Kamakura Period seed storage jars of dark clay were made. The density and high shrinkage of the clay necessitated an unusually long firing period, and this resulted in the wares becoming a dark reddish black with a heavy ash glaze deposit. These old wares were collected by the tea masters and used in the tea ceremony as water pots, often fitted with lacquer lids.

From the mid-fifteenth century models of birds and animals were produced. The

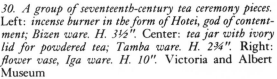

30. *A group of seventeenth-century tea ceremony pieces.* Left: *incense burner in the form of Hotei, god of contentment; Bizen ware. H. 3½".* Center: *tea jar with ivory lid for powdered tea; Tamba ware. H. 2¾".* Right: *flower vase, Iga ware. H. 10".* Victoria and Albert Museum

bodies were made of a fine clay and covered with a dark brown glaze, the finished pieces resembling bronze.

In the Momoyama Period tea ceremony wares such as flower vases, tea jars, water containers, and incense burners (Ill. 30) were made, but the clay was not considered suitable for teabowls.

Today the Bizen kilns produce bricks and drainpipes.

Bizen wares generally carry a mark; the most familiar modern mark is a cherry blossom.

Tamba: Tamba pottery was made in the villages of Oji, Muramori, Inahata, Kamaya, Onobara, and Tachikui, in Tamba Province, to the northwest of Kyoto.

The old wares were limited to a few shapes; large storage jars and sake bottles are the most common forms. The local clay, which has long since been used up, was coarse, and when fired became a dark red brown or gray brown color (Ill. 10). The clay was used much as it was dug from the ground, just wet down and kneaded into coils for use on a slowly revolving wheel. The wares were not glazed before firing, and the natural ash glaze, *bidoro*, was often very thick on account of the long firing necessitated by the type of kiln then in use. This was the *ana-gama*, the cave kiln.

About 1600 Korean-style "split bamboo" kilns were built. They were made of brick, in a shape resembling a split bamboo pole. The long tube was partially buried in the slope of a hill, with about one third of it above the level of the ground. These kilns were more efficient and the firing was accomplished in a much shorter time. Three different types of glazes were used—black, red brown, and amber. Production of the older forms continued, the wares becoming more regular and symmetrical, but new shapes were also introduced, notably the tea jar for storing tea leaves with its four ears for tying on the lid. Kobori Enshū visited Tamba and ordered tea jars to be made for his use. Tea jars to hold powdered tea were also made (Ill. 30).

In the early part of the nineteenth century slip-decorated ware was made at Tamba, but this production was short-lived and died out before the Meiji Period. At the beginning of this century sake bottles were also made at Tamba in large quantities.

In the early 1930s the jigger wheel made its appearance. However, the old hand methods continued to be used side by side with the new.

Modern Tamba wares have a chocolate, mahogany-colored, or blue black glaze, often splashed with yellow, over a red brown body. Another type of modern ware is decorated with simple designs in colored enamels on an unglazed gray body. Clays are brought from elsewhere, as the local clays are exhausted. The Tamba potters use the coil-and-throw method for all larger shapes, starting with a clay disk or slab for the base.

There are over twenty kilns in use at Tachikui at the present time, and although all are of the same type, they are different from any others now in use in Japan. They appear to be survivals and adaptations of the old climbing kilns.

Shigaraki: The Shigaraki kiln sites lie in an area between Kyoto and Seto, a little to the south. There is a legend that Korean potters settled there in the twelfth century.

The wares have a rough, unsophisticated appearance (Ill. 31). The clays, with their high sand and gravel content, cannot be thrown on the wheel, and the coil method has been used down to this day. The typical

31. Shigaraki ware grain storage jar. Muromachi Period (1333–1568). Private Collection

Shigaraki body, gray with coarse granules of partially fired quartz protruding from it, is covered with a natural glaze. The early wares were strictly utilitarian; seed jars, water vats, and grating mortars are the most common types of vessels. In the sixteenth

and seventeenth centuries the tea masters patronized the kilns, using the smaller wares as flower vases or water jars, and also ordering wares made to their own taste.

Today the same type of ware is still being produced, but artificial glazes are used.

Iga: The Iga and Shigaraki kilns are situated on the same mountain range, the Shigaraki kilns on the northern slopes and the Iga kilns on the southern. Up to the sixteenth century the wares of the two areas were very similar, but in later times a viscous, white-bodied clay was used at the Iga kilns.

Furuta Oribe visited Iga at the beginning of the seventeenth century and under his influence Iga began to make tea ceremony wares.

The typical Iga wares have a cracked or split gray body, which is usually distorted (Ill. 30). The natural glaze of brown, gray, and green on the old wares came to the surface when the clay was fired, but today artificial glazes are used here too. The older wares were admired for their roughness and natural flaws, but as time went on the potters learned to contrive these effects, with the consequent self-conscious artificiality.

Enshū's Seven Favorite Kilns

Kobori Enshū, whose real name was Kobori Totomi-no-Kami Masakuzu, was a tea master who served under Ieyasu. A follower of the style of Sen-no-Rikyū, he preferred a polished and tranquil type of ware that was made at a number of kilns in Japan. These kilns, known as Enshū's Seven Favorite Kilns, are Shidoro, Zeze, Kosobe, Agano, Takatori, Asahi, and Akahada. With the exception of Kosobe, all the kilns are still in production today, and there is a movement to rebuild the Kosobe.

Shidoro wares are undecorated; the glaze on the stoneware body is of a rich brown, similar to the Ko-Seto glazes. The kiln was established in 1575 by Kato Shoyemon Kagetada.

Kosobe wares were unknown until 1625, when they were popularized by Enshū. They have a fine hard body, and the

32. Top, at left: *teacup, Asahi, 1880.* Center: *wine cup, Sakurai, 1875.* Right: *bowl, Kosobe, 1875.* Peabody Museum of Salem Morse Collection; Photograph by Y. W. Sexton. Top, right: *tea jar, Zeze ware; early eighteenth century.* Private Collection. Left: *Teabowl, Akahada ware, Yamato Province.* Courtesy Museum of Fine Arts, Boston; Morse Collection

glazes range from white to a dark gray. They are often decorated with a few brush-strokes in brown (Ill. 32).

Zeze wares have a golden or red brown and purple glaze over a dark gray fine-grained biscuit. The kiln was established in 1630 under the direction of Enshū (Ill. 32).

Agano wares were at first Korean in style, but later became more like Takatori wares. The later wares have a bluish green glaze. The kiln was started in 1602.

Takatori wares have either a black brown glaze or combinations of white and dark glazes. The kilns were established by Koreans at the foot of the Takatori mountain about 1600.

The Asahi kiln was founded in 1600, and in 1645 Okumura Tosaku, under En-shū's supervision, made teabowls of light brown or light blue glaze on a coarse biscuit. The name Asahi, which means "morning sun," is said to be derived from the color of the ware. Between 1830 and 1873 modern wares were produced by a potter named Chobei Matsubayashi.

Akahada wares made for the tea ceremony under Enshū's direction resemble Takatori ware, with a grayish white glaze (Ill. 32). The kiln was started in 1580, but then ceased operation until it was revived in 1645 by Nonomura Ninsei. It closed again and was reopened later, the best wares of its later period being made by Mokuhaku (1799–1870). Many of Mokuhaku's pieces are copies of Ninsei's wares, but he also made teabowls with designs showing Horai, the Taoist land of the immortals, and water jars with pictures in the style of Buddhist scrolls of the Nara Period.

Karatsu

Wares made in the Karatsu area during the first half of the sixteenth century were the first true ceramic wares to be made in

33. Kiln waster, Karatsu ware. Nineteenth century. Philadelphia Museum of Art, given by Theodore T. Newbold; Photograph by A. J. Wyatt

Kyushu. The name Karatsu means literally "China port"; the port of Karatsu lies just across the Tsushima Strait from Korea. Korean potters at Karatsu built Korean-type sloping kilns, and the wares they made were almost identical to those made at the same time in southern Korea. These wares were made by the coiling method, beaten into shape with paddles, and decorated with a dark brown iron glaze.

The Karatsu kilns made both utility and tea ceremony wares. Many pieces originally intended for everyday use by the peasants were taken by the tea masters for use in the tea ceremony.

Karatsu were made in a number of different types. Those covered with a plain ash slip glaze are called Muji-*garatsu*, or undecorated Karatsu; wares with painted designs in underglaze iron are called *E-garatsu*

(decorated Karatsu), and the designs depict trees, plants, floral patterns, and birds (Ills. 14 and 33). *Temmoku* Karatsu has a black glaze; *Madara-garatsu* (spotted, or mottled, Karatsu) has a devitrified white glaze over the feldspar-clay ground, whereas *Korai-garatsu*, or Korean Karatsu, is glazed partly in white and partly in an amber color. Wares were also made in Oribe style.

Hagi

The kilns at Hagi in the province of Nagate were also begun by naturalized Korean potters. The kilns were built about 1600 and produced tea ceremony wares during the first part of the seventeenth century. These wares have a crackled grayish white glaze.

Banko

In the middle of the nineteenth century a Karatsu-type ware was made at the Banko kiln in the province of Isé. We are told by Augustus Franks that in 1850 Yusetsu, a native of the village of Obuke, near Kuwana, in Isé, founded a factory at Kuwana.

During the seventeenth century Banko Kichibei had established a kiln on the outskirts of Edo, but the existence of this kiln was quite short-lived. Mori Yusetsu had dis-covered Banko Kichibei's receipts for glazes and enamels among his father's stock—his father was a dealer in waste paper—and after studying these, decided to become a potter. He bought the Banko seal from a grandson of the original potter, took the name of Banko for himself, and started work at Kuwana (Ill. 34).

The Banko factory is still in existence; it is well known for small teapots of reddish brown stoneware. The lids usually have decorative small knobs in the shape of animals.

34. Two Banko ware pieces: Left, *flower vase, 1875.* Victoria and Albert Museum, London. Right, *jar, 1870.* Metropolitan Museum of Art, New York

5

Arita and Imari

The village of Arita is about fifty miles north of Nagasaki. Ri-Sampei, a Korean, first founded a porcelain factory there in the early seventeenth century, and ever since that time other porcelain makers have gathered there, making it a great center of the industry. Ri-Sampei discovered good materials at Idsumi-yama, a hill near the valley in which Arita is situated, in the county of Matsuara. The official catalog of the Japanese section of the Centennial Exposition of 1876 in Philadelphia states:

Within a very limited circuit (of Arita), not half a mile in diameter, there are found imbedded in the rock at different places, all the materials necessary for the glaze, for the "craquelé" etc., the best being of such good quality, that after being powdered and decanted, it is used without any further mixture for the finest ware, the so-called egg-shell porcelain.

The Lord Nabeshima, who governed the district until the revolution, appointed an official to act as overseer of the quarrying, and this man set up a gate on the road to prevent unauthorized persons from entering and removing materials from the quarries. After 1868, this system of control was abolished and the clay was needlessly wasted. The first porcelain wares to be produced were in underglaze blue and white *(sometsuke)*, with decoration in a great variety of patterns and motifs: landscapes, flow- ers, birds, fish, animals, human figures, and geometrical designs.

Kakiemon

Kakiemon I (1596–1666) is generally credited with being the first Japanese potter to apply overglaze enamels successfully to porcelain (Ills. 15 and 35).

Born Sakaida Kizaiemon, the first Kakiemon was the son of Sakaida Ensai, a native of Kakaida in Fujioka Prefecture. Ensai is reputed to have been a man of some social standing who wrote poetry. The family moved to Shiraishi in Hizen, there becoming tile makers. Then they moved to Nangawara, near Arita, where Ensai and his son learned from a Chinese potter how to make blue and white porcelain.

Although Kakiemon's name and reputation are based entirely on his enameled porcelain, he probably did not begin to produce these wares until he was about fifty, and another ten years elapsed before he found the secret of applying gold. According to tradition, he came into contact in Arita with a pottery merchant named Tokuyemon, who had learned the art of overglaze enameling from a Chinese potter in Nagasaki. Tokuyemon in turn taught Kakiemon, and together they experimented to perfect the art. An old document in the Kakiemon family says that in the following year, "the year of the galleon" (i.e., the year the Dutch galleon came (1646), Tokuyemon took the

35. Dish, Kakiemon ware, Arita. Seventeenth century. Kakiemon I was the first Japanese potter to use overglaze enamels successfully on porcelain. As he and his two sons worked side by side making these decorated wares, the work of the three is very similar. Metropolitan Museum of Art, Rogers Fund

enameled pieces to Nagasaki, where he sold them to the Dutch and Chinese as well as to the agent of Maeda Toshitune, lord of Kaga. Another traditional version says that Maeda Toshitune founded the kiln at Kutani, and sent Goto Saijiro to learn the secrets of enameling porcelain from Kakiemon in Arita.

Brinkley's well-known version, in his *Japan, Its History, Arts and Literature,* is that Tokuyemon and Kakiemon set out in 1646 to visit China to learn the secrets of overglaze enamel decoration on porcelain. However, in Nagasaki, they made the acquaintance of the master of a Chinese junk, who was able to supply them with the necessary information, and so instead of continuing their journey to China, they returned to Arita. In view of the dire penalties meted out to anyone who went abroad, or even took shorter excursions, as exemplified in the fate of Goto Saijiro in Kutani (see Chapter 7), this story seems most unlikely.

There are two traditional versions of how Kakiemon acquired his art name. The family kiln at Nangawara was in the domain of the lords of Nabeshima, and one version is that when Sakaida Kizaiemon made a *tokonama* decoration *(okimono)* in the form of two red persimmons *(kaki)* and presented it to Nabeshima Katsushigi, the daimyo was so pleased with it that he gave its maker the name of Kakiemon. The other version is that the name was derived from the persimmon red color of the overglaze he used.

Kakiemon was the first potter to produce designs in the Japanese style of simplicity and blank spaces, known as *yamato-e,* in contrast to the crowded Chinese style of decoration that covered the entire surface. His patterns rarely covered more than one third to one half the surface to be decorated, thereby contrasting with and enchancing the beauty of the cream white body and glaze. The patterns, very light and delicate in nature, often with no apparent outline, are generally of flowers, birds, or butterflies, naturalistically painted. A characteristic of the wares is a line of iron red glazing around the edge called *kuchi-beni* (mouth rouge).

The colors used are mainly a soft orange red, the color of a ripe persimmon, and an azure blue, along with a pale yellow, lavender blue, purple, grass green, and black, all sparingly applied. Some pieces have gold highlights, but gold is never used for lavish display as on Imari wares.

The designs are outlined in black or red (for the red and yellow sections). The black is a fine brushstroke of cobalt, but as it was applied on the glaze after the firing, it failed to turn blue. Nabeshima designs were also outlined in cobalt, but since they were drawn directly on the unglazed biscuit, the subsequent high temperature firing brought out the blue.

Kakiemon porcelain wares were always of the best quality and made by expert craftsmen, in contrast to Imari porcelains, which were produced for export and for everyday use. The clay used for the body was far superior to that used for Imari, and the pieces underwent two bakings before enameling, the first firing for the under-glazed milk white porcelain bodies, called *nigoshi-de,* and the second for the very thin glaze.

Kakiemon wares were exported to Europe by way of the Dutch settlement at Nagasaki during the second half of the seventeenth century. Along with the so-called old Imari wares, they exerted a tremendous influence on European taste and resulting porcelain production in Europe.

Vestiges of huge European collections of old Japanese wares can still be seen in many countries. In England Queen Mary II collected Japanese porcelain. Although born an English princess, she lived for some years in Holland with her consort William of Orange (who became William III of England) before they were called to England in 1686 to take up the succession, and so she was in Holland during the time when the importation of Japanese wares was at its height. It is interesting to note that her collection includes many fine pieces of Kakiemon, some of which may still be seen at Hampton Court. The first mention of Kak-

iemon ware in the Dutch East India Company inventory was in 1684, and therefore Queen Mary must have been among the first to collect this ware.

Kakiemon porcelain imported at that time is also to be found in English country houses of the same period. Whether Queen Mary's collection had anything to do with the appreciation of these wares in England is a matter for speculation, but her collection was much admired; John Evelyn remarked on it in his diary more than once.

The largest collection of Japanese porcelains was at Dresden, accumulated by Augustus the Strong and installed in the "Japanese Palace." It is a later collection than Queen Mary's, much of it having been bought in 1715 and 1717. The collection was moved to the Johanneum in 1875 and opened to the public the following year, but through subsequent sales, as well as disastrous losses during the Second World War, just a small proportion remains, including only about twenty pieces of Kakiemon.

In France the Prince of Condé assembled a collection of Kakiemon wares between 1735 and 1740, and other collections may be found throughout Europe. The Baroque palaces of Germany, Austria, Hungary, and Sweden, St. James's Palace and Windsor Castle in England, as well as country houses in those countries, all have their share, although the origin of the Japanese pieces was not always recognized. In a Dresden inventory of 1721 there is a note saying that Augustus the Strong was in the habit of calling Kakiemon ware "Old Indian Ware," and old inventories of English country houses speak of "China ware" or even "Old East Indian ware."

Kakiemon porcelain was so well liked that soon copies were being made everywhere. The first were the Japanese copies, starting about 1672, when the secrets of overglaze enameling began to be generally known. They were made at kilns around Arita and at Kutani, many of them being almost impossible to distinguish from wares made at the Kakiemon kiln, although none of them have the fine milk white body of the originals.

Fast on the heels of these came the Chinese copies, made soon after 1700. The Chi-

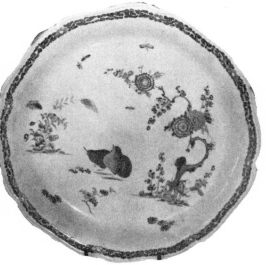

36. *Three pieces made at Bow, England, c. 1755. Quail design, showing Kakiemon influence.* Private Collection; Photograph by V. R. Pepper

nese pieces usually have underglaze blue in place of the overglaze blue enamel of the originals. They were probably made for export to Europe to compete with the Japanese pieces. But copies were soon being made in Europe too. Since Kakiemon is fairly simple and naturalistic in decoration, it was much easier to copy than the more complicated Chinese designs.

The earliest European copies were made at the Meissen factory near Dresden, the first being produced about 1728. France followed suit shortly afterward in the 1730s. Dutch enamelers were also soon busily decorating porcelain blanks imported "in the white" from Japan and China.

English decorators copied from the Meissen versions, rather than from the origi-

nal Kakiemon pieces. Chelsea produced some pieces between 1749 and 1752 bearing the raised anchor mark, but many more are to be found with the red anchor mark (1752–1756). Bow made copies during the 1750s (Ill. 36), and Worcester followed closely thereafter.

The Kakiemon family has continued to make fine porcelain wares down to the present day. It is now in its thirteenth generation.

The wares of the first three Kakiemon are very similar, the father and sons working together side by side. Kakiemon IV and Kakiemon V both died young, and the wares they produced were not as fine as those of their predecessors. A revival took place in the time of Kakiemon VI, under his uncle's direction, and wares produced during this period are considered by the Japanese to be among the finest. Kakiemon VII, who marked his wares with the *fuku* (good fortune) mark in a double square, continued to make wares in the same tradition, but they are not regarded as particularly notable. Kakiemon VIII used the *saki-kaki* mark (the wine persimmon mark). Kakiemon IX (1776–1836) and Kakiemon X (1805–1860) produced mostly blue and white wares.

Kakiemon XI, called Shibonsuke (1845–1917), worked in the traditional style and generally used the *fuku* mark in a double square. However, during the Meiji era, when the traditional arts were pushed aside and forgotten in the wild pursuit of Western ideas, the family became very poor and had to sell their mark. Kakiemon XII (born 1879) continued the traditional art, as does his son Kakiemon XIII, who assumed his title in March 1963.

The porcelains being produced by the present members of the family are still of the highest quality, and are relatively expensive when compared to the modern Imari wares. The body is made from a blend of three types of porcelain stone from the mountains in the Arita area. This stone is carefully selected. After being crushed, screened, and mixed, only about 30 percent of it is considered good enough to be used. The resulting wares are very fine copies of the old ones, hard to distinguish from the originals.

Imari Wares

The name Imari ware covers porcelain made at a number of different kilns and exported from the port of Imari. The kilns

37. Blue and white porcelain bottle, Imari ware, Arita. Seventeenth century. Courtesy of the Brooklyn Museum, Carll H. De Silver Fund

were at Arita (with six branch kilns at Ichinose, Hirose, Nagawara, Ou-he, Hokao, Kuromuta), and at Okawaji, Shira-ishi, Shida, Koshida, Yoshia, and Matsugaya. Although Imari ware was exported in large quantities to Europe, where it exerted great influence on porcelain manufacture there, it was never solely an export ware. It has always been popular in Japan, but less so than Kutani ware, and the pieces are of a more common nature.

The first pieces were in blue and white (Ill. 37). Although Kakiemon was the first Japanese potter to work successfully in overglaze enamels, the secret soon spread to other potters in the Arita area, and they also began to decorate with overglaze enamels. These wares were first called *aka-e*, or red painted wares, in contrast to *gosu*, or blue and white, even though they included blue and white decoration.

38. Dishes, Arita. Nineteenth century. Metropolitan Museum of Art, Gift of Charles Stewart Smith

39. *Armorial dish, Arita ware. Eighteenth century. A similar piece, from the British Museum, is shown in Soame Jenyns's* Japanese Porcelain. *He identifies the coat of arms as that of the Portuguese family of Brandao, quartered with the arms of the Carvalhais and Vasconcelos families.* Philadelphia Museum of Art; Photograph by A. J. Wyatt

Old documents of the year 1662 mention the *aka-e machi* ("red picture street," or street of enamelers), which was part of the main street in Arita. There were eleven houses of porcelain decorators on the street; these artists added enamel overglaze colors to the blue and white wares brought to them. The style of decoration they used was developed to please the Dutch market.

The first overglaze enamel wares were in three colors, but other colors were soon added (Ills. 38 and 39). For the period we are surveying here, the following categories will suffice:

1. *sometsuke:* underglaze blue and white
2. *sansai:* three color or Old Japan
3. *nishikide:* brocade Imari
4. *kinrande:* gold designs on a red enamel ground

Sometsuke wares can be found in a great variety of patterns and motifs, although flowers, birds, fish, and animals were the most popular in the later period.

Imari *sansai,* or old Japan wares, are decorated in underglaze blue with overglaze red on a white ground, the designs being highlighted in gold. Most of the surface is covered with decoration, both inside and out. A basket of flowers is a very popular central motif on these wares (Ill. 40).

Imari *nishikide,* or brocade Imari, uses more colors. Originally it was copied from the five color wares of the late Ming and early Ching dynasties of China. The Japanese call any mass of brilliant colors a "brocade," the name being derived from this practice rather than from any resemblance to actual brocades. The designs cover almost all the surface, with hardly any ground glaze left visible. The colors chiefly used are underglaze blue and overglaze enamels in brick red, gold, turquoise green, lemon yellow, and purple.

Imari *kinrande,* or gold-on-red Imari, employs gold Chinese-style designs on the typical Imari red background (Ill. 44). Kutani wares also have gold decoration on a red ground, but the Imari and Kutani reds

40. Late nineteenth century Imari sansai, or old Japan ware. Blue underglaze with red overglaze enamel, highlighted in gold. The basket of flowers in the center is a transfer. The poor quality blotchy decoration must have been made at high speed for the flourishing export market. Beware of Imari wares of this period; some pieces leave much to be desired.

41. Imari nishikide, or brocade Imari, plate. Late nineteenth or early twentieth century. D. 9".

42. Imari bowl, late nineteenth century. Philadelphia Museum of Art; Photograph by A. J. Wyatt

43. Imari nishikide. D. 12". Underglaze blue with red, green, and yellow decoration. Early twentieth century.

44. Plate, Imari kinrande, or gold-on-red Imari. Chinese-style gold designs (Chinese grass) with green flowers on red background. Five variously shaped reserves with underglaze blue patterns, highlighted in gold. Twentieth century. Pinney Collection

are quite different (see Color Plates 8 and 11).

A decorative pattern of symbols in underglaze blue is usually found around the rim on the underside of Imari plates and platters. Those most frequently used are the symbols of the eight Chinese Treasures, which are called *happo*, or *hachi ho*, in Japanese. They consist of a gold coin, two books, stone chimes, artemisia leaf, dragon pearl, lozenge, mirror, and rhinoceros horns (Fig. 2).

Imari wares have been made in the same tradition for the last two hundred years, but the general age of a piece is usually fairly

decoration intended to please the barbarian taste of foreigners. Morse's remarks in *Japan Day by Day,* quoted in Chapter 8, could have applied just as well to Imari. The haste and "sickening profusion" of the splashed-on decoration is as evident here as on Awata wares. Not all Imari wares of this period were badly done, however, and the collector has to exercise his own judgment when making a purchase.

In this century all kinds of Imari wares have been exported—good, bad, and indifferent. The good has some very fine deco-

Fig. 2. *The eight Chinese Treasures, often used as decoration on the underside of modern Imari wares* (left to right, from top): *gold coin, dragon pearl, lozenge, two books, mirror, stone chimes, artemisia leaf, and rhinoceros horns.*

evident. As is true of all the other types of Japanese ceramics, the workmanship was finer and more painstaking before the Meiji era. Imari ware suffered more than any other at the outset of the Meiji era, probably because the brilliant colors readily lent themselves to making dreadful daubs of

ration, and the biscuit is also of good quality. The bad is of the cheap dime-store variety. The Imari wares produced since World War II are of good quality, but in my opinion the type of decoration lends itself too much to mechanical reproduction, so that the charm of the older wares is lost. Unfortunately, the

45. Imari plate, twentieth century, probably made in the 1930s. Poor quality decoration.

perfection of the machine is the antithesis of art, and no matter how beautiful a design may be, unless there is a touch of human imperfection, there is no art. Late nineteenth-century Imari wares have a warmth that, even in their badness, seems preferable to the coldness of perfection.

As a broad indication of dates, the following may be useful. If the foot rim of a piece is worn smooth through much use, the piece is old. If a piece carries a potter's mark, it was almost certainly made after 1868. If the underglaze blue is in cobalt oxide, the piece was made after 1869, the year that im-ported oxidized cobalt was first used at Arita. Oxidized cobalt is a brighter blue than the native cobalt and is characterized by a much more even application (see Color Plates 6 and 8).

Very bad blotchy decoration would seem to indicate that a piece was made in the first half of the Meiji era. If made on a jigger, the piece probably dates after 1915, and if the piece is very large, it was most likely made after the mid-twenties (Ill. 46). A description of the jigger and how to detect clues indicating its use are given in Chapter 13.

46. Large trencher, D. 18″. Imari nishikide. Twentieth century. Well made, with several colors; delicately painted.

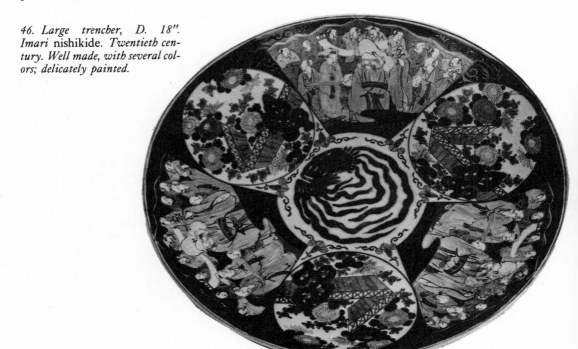

Nabeshima Wares

Nabeshima ware was originally made exclusively for Lord Nabeshima, feudal lord of the Arita region, after whom it was named. It was made either for his own use or for him to give to his friends. Since these wares were not made for the commercial market, little was known about them outside Japan until 1867, when some pieces were sent to the International Exposition in Paris.

The Imaizumi family, who still practice their traditional art, were the decorators of this fine porcelain. The older Nabeshima ware is generally considered to be the best porcelain ever made in Japan, the body being a pure white, with a slight bluish tinge. The only other wares that approach the perfection of the Nabeshima are the Hirado, but they were not made in the same styles.

A very high standard of production has always prevailed. In the early days only about 10 percent of the pieces were considered perfect enough for use, the poorest being discarded; even now, about half are still discarded. Clay molds were used so that the pieces would be uniform in shape.

There is a considerable difference of opinion about the date of the founding of the Nabeshima factory with imported Korean potters; dates vary from 1624 to 1672. It is generally believed that the factory was moved in 1675 to its site at Okawachi, which lies in the mountains about eight miles north of Arita. In the eighteenth century the pieces were made and biscuit fired at Okawachi. Then they were brought by retainers of the Nabeshima clan to the Imaizumi family, who lived on the *aka-e machi* in Arita, for decoration. During the decorating and subsequent firing the house was guarded by Nabeshima samurai, who marched back with the completed wares to the clan castle in the mountains.

The original Nabeshima ware was blue and white; then some celadons were made, and in the early eighteenth century *Iro-Nabeshima*, or colored Nabeshima, came into being. The colors used, which resemble watercolors, were underglaze blue, a bright soft red, a soft green, a pale yellow, and a thin purple (Ills. 47 and 48).

What is truly remarkable and unique about Nabeshima ware in comparison with all other ceramic wares produced in Japan at

47. Plate, Nabeshima ware; nineteenth century. Courtesy of the Museum of Fine Arts, Boston, Bigelow Collection

48. *Plate, Nabeshima ware; nineteenth century.* Metropolitan Museum of Art, Gift of Mrs. V. Everit Macy.

that time is that the decoration on each piece of a set is exactly the same, as if it had been printed. The method the Nabeshima potters used to transfer the pattern was as follows: First, they drew the design on a piece of tissue paper with gourd charcoal; then they put the paper on the inside of the dish to be decorated, and rubbed it to transfer the pattern onto the biscuit. The process was repeated on all the pieces of the set. The outlines of the pattern were then drawn in *gosu* (cobalt), and the biscuit firing developed the pattern outlines in blue and white, ready for the overglaze enamels.

The age of Nabeshima ware is generally determined by the exactness of the application of the overglaze enamels to the underglaze outlines; the later pieces are not as carefully done. The patterns became much more crowded on nineteenth-century pieces, but the traditional designs have continued to be used by the family down through the

years; new pieces bear the same patterns. The most characteristic pieces are the plates or dishes on a high base, called *takadaizara* (Ill. 49) decorated with a comb-tooth pattern in blue and white. On the early wares the comb-tooth design was perfectly regular, but nineteenth- and twentieth-century pieces lack this regularity.

On the underside of the dishes is a "treasures" pattern in three places, transferred by the same tissue paper method. This placing of patterns on the underside is copied from the traditional style of Chinese porcelain from the Ming and later periods.

The Imaizumi family were the only enamel workers in Arita who had clan protection; all the other decorators worked commercially. In 1871 the clan system was abolished, and the Imaizumi started to work on their own. They began to make their own clay bodies and fired them in a cooperative kiln. About 1890 they built their own

49. *Nabeshima dish, nineteenth century, showing the high base called* takadaizara, *with comb-tooth design.* Captain and Mrs. Roger Gerry

50. *Nabeshima dish, Meiji Period (1868–1912), made by Imaizumi Imaemon in Arita.* Philadelphia Museum of Art, given by Mrs. Herbert C. Morris. Photograph by A. J. Wyatt

51. Footed dishes, Hirado ware; nineteenth century. Philadelphia Museum of Art, given by Mrs. Edgar Stone; Photograph by A. J. Wyatt

kiln, but this proved unsuccessful and they lost money and had to sell their house in 1897.

The twelfth generation, Imaizumi Imaemon, however, studied ceramics at the industrial school in Arita, and spent four years studying kiln construction and firing. After completing his studies he was able to construct a small one-chamber kiln, which enabled the family to produce Nabeshima wares successfully once again (Ill. 50).

The wares now being produced are of fine quality in refined taste—technically, almost equal to the old specimens.

Hirado Wares

Like Imari, Hirado wares derive their name from the place of export, not from the site of the kilns. The Mikawachi factory, situated in the village of Use, about six miles south of Arita, was a private factory of the prince of Hirado from 1751 to 1843. Only after the middle of the nineteenth century were the wares on the open market and exported from the port of Hirado (Ill. 51).

Under the patronage of the Matsuura family, princes of Hirado, the Mikawachi kilns produced some very fine porcelain. These pieces were unmarked. After 1843, when a lower grade of wares was produced, the pieces carried a mark.

Hirado wares are famous for their fine milk white porcelain bodies, intricate modeling, and the delicacy of the decoration on the blue and white pieces. Brinkley tells us that the stone for the body was brought from Amakusa, and that not more than five or six feet in every hundred were used; the stone was laboriously pulverized and strained. Satsuma ash was imported at great expense and mixed with the Amakusa stone, the resulting paste being milk white and as fine as pipe clay. The glaze was equally pure and smooth, with a velvety luster.

In the *sometsuke* the underglaze decoration is in a pale delicate blue of a distinctive soft quality, the cobalt being imported from China (Ill. 52). The exquisitely painted designs include landscapes, flowers, and trees, as well as the popular motif of Chinese boys playing under a pine tree. The number of boys depicted depended on the quality of the ware—the best had seven boys, the next had five, and the ordinary ware had only three.

This type of ware is still being produced today. The body is of the finest quality, and the decorations are very carefully done.

Another type of Mikawachi porcelain ware was ornamented with designs in relief. This decoration was produced by painting with a brush dipped in slip.

52. Jar, Hirado ware, c. 1870. Metropolitan Museum of Art, Macy Collection, Gift of Mrs. V. Everit Macy

Eggshell porcelain, a paper-thin glossy translucent porcelain enameled in various colors, was used to make small pieces for export from the mid-nineteenth century onward. Augustus Franks tells us in his *Japanese Pottery* that the pieces were turned on the potter's wheel, and the material used, which came from the island of Amakusa, or Goto, was softer and tougher than that from Id-sumi-yama.

The Japanese collection at the Philadelphia Centennial Exposition in 1876 included a teacup with handle and a saucer, both of European form, in eggshell porcelain. They were painted in red with gilding, and had six oblong white panels, each of which contained a figure of a poet. These pieces were made expressly for the Philadelphia Exposition. (See Ill. 78 for a similar decoration on Kutani pieces.)

Hirado wares also include small ornamental objects such as charming models of children, animals, swans, or branches of flowering shrubs.

6

Kyoto

Kyoto was the western capital, the city of the emperor and his court for almost eleven hundred years. From the eighth century, when it was founded by the Emperor Kammu and called Heian, through the civil wars, when it was almost razed, through the splendor of the Momoyama Period of the sixteenth century, to the Meiji Restoration in 1868, it remained a city of culture and refinement.

Beauty and good taste were to be found everywhere; artists of all kinds considered the quiet dreamy atmosphere of the old capital stimulating. It inspired the soft refined beauty of their ceramic wares, so the Japanese tell us. Kenzan's friend and patron, Prince Rinnoji-no-miya, said that even the nightingales sang more sweetly in Kyoto than in Edo.

A Kyoto accent was considered to be the indication of a cultivated person, because of its association with the court and literature. After the shogunate had been established in Edo at the beginning of the seventeenth century and the emperor had no more political authority, the court devoted its attention to poetry, music, and the fine arts, with the result that Kyoto became the cultural center of the country.

Craftsmen had been producing exquisite articles for the court since the city was first built, using as their inspiration all the beautiful things imported by the aristocracy from China and other parts of Asia. Even

after the government had passed to Edo, Kyoto still remained the center of production for luxury articles.

In the sixteenth century Kyoto was the chief mercantile city of Japan, although it was not a seaport. Kyoto-owned ships sailed all over the eastern Pacific, going even as far as Siam, and the goods they carried were transported between Kyoto and the ports of Sai and Osaka by way of the Yodo River. After the country was closed to foreign trade in the seventeenth century, memories remained and influenced the arts produced there.

Kyoto's narrow streets could be covered by drawing canvas blinds across from one side to the other, keeping off the hot summer sun and providing welcome shade in the humid heat. Some streets had arcades to shelter shoppers from the sun and rain; bamboo curtains hung from the arcades protected the shops from dust. Each shop also had a curtain (*noren*) in front of its door, the curtain being decorated with an animal, symbol, or a number to identify the shop. Traditional potters, whose families run into many generations, are called *noren* potters, a name derived from this curtain with the family crest on it.

Shutters on the street side of a shop could be raised or slid aside to reveal the shopkeeper and his assistants sitting amid their goods on a raised area covered with *tatami* (a pressed rice-straw mat overlaid with woven rushes). The customer did not enter the *tatami* area, but did his shopping from the edge of the street.

Some type of handicraft was carried on in nearly every house in the city, and members of the same trade lived side by side on certain streets. Where the Tokaido, the old road from Edo (Tokyo), entered the city at Awataguchi, there were kilns for baking pottery. Other potters settled in various areas around the capital, and to this day there is a street of potters (Teapot Lane) on the hillside near Kiyomizu.

Kyoto wares hold the distinction of having been marked with the potter's name or seal from early days, in contrast to wares from other kilns, which are known by their kiln name. The Kyoto potter was an individual artist operating his private kiln; and an artist was a man to be respected. Not only did he have his own style of decoration, but the blend of clays he used was individual as well. Unlike the Arita area, where there were large deposits of clay in a state ready to be used, in Kyoto potters had to use clays brought from other places, and these clays had to be blended together to be workable. Each potter created his own particular blend. Individual Kyoto potters have a long history of working each in his own style, a tradition that continues unbroken today.

Kyoto wares fall into three main types: Raku ware, Awata ware, and Kiyomizu ware, the two last together called Ninsei ware.

Raku Wares

Raku wares have been made in Kyoto since 1580. Today there are two distinct branches of potters making Raku-*yaki*. The *hon-gama* (principal kiln) is the legitimate line of successors to the Raku seal; the family name of these potters is Tanaka, and they are now in their fourteenth generation. The *wake-gama*, or branch kilns, are operated by potters working in the Raku style in a number of areas.

The first maker of these wares was called Chōjirō (1516–1595); he was the son of a Korean potter who settled in Kyoto and made roof tiles. The making of roof tiles was an important industry in Kyoto. Houses were constructed of wood, and in consequence there were frequent disastrous fires. During the seventeenth century edicts were issued that all the houses in town had to be built with tile roofs.

Chōjirō and his brother Jokei made roof tiles for the Shogun Hideyoshi's pleasure pavilion, the *ju-raku-tei*, and Rikyū, Hideyoshi's favorite tea master, had them make some utensils for the tea ceremony. As a great honor Rikyū gave Chōjirō his own old family name of Tanaka, having himself been given the new family name of Sen by Hideyoshi. Chōjirō is considered the first generation of the Raku line of potters, although Hideyoshi gave the seal with the character "raku" to Chōjirō's brother Jokei, who is known as the second generation. Jokei adopted Raku as a family name.

The legitimate successor to a line of potters is the one to whom the present holder of the title entrusts the secrets of his art. These are never written down, but bequeathed orally either to a son, if there is one capable of holding the succession, or to a promising pupil. This practice can create considerable confusion for the historian, as some families appear to have had an amazing number of generations in a few short years.

Raku ware is a soft, light, thickly glazed type of pottery, essentially the product of small family kilns. When Edward Morse visited the twelfth Raku, he noted that the oven used for the teabowls was so small it could hold only one bowl at a time. The bowls are baked at a low temperature, the firing being similar to that used in tile making.

The wares are formed in two different ways. One is by coiling, thin ropes of clay being coiled around and built up into the shape of the bowl. The foot rim is a separate coil placed at the base, the whole being smoothed with the fingers, but the coils always being apparent. The other way is to form the bowl with the fingers from a lump of clay, and to shape and refine it with the aid of a bamboo spatula.

The irregularities that make each piece individual are the prized qualities in Raku ware. The marks of the bamboo cutting

53. Two Raku ware pottery teabowls, with bamboo tea whisk. Meiji Period. Philadelphia Museum of Art, teabowls given by Mrs. John Reilly through Mrs. William Henry Fox; tea whisk given by Y. Hattori of Kyoto; Photograph by A. J. Wyatt

knife are deeply appreciated; the uneven surface, unsymmetrical shape, and varied color are other distinctive qualities.

The teabowl had to have walls thick enough not to conduct the heat so that the bowl could be held comfortably in the hands, but it also had to keep the tea hot at the same time. The thick soft walls of Raku ware perform this task admirably. The bowl must also fit the hands comfortably—it is never a perfect round, and the rim must not be straight, lest it feel unyielding to the mouth.

A portion near the base of a teabowl is always left unglazed so that the material forming the body may be seen and appreciated; the clays used are mostly the iron-bearing clays of Kyoto. There are a number of points to be considered when judging teabowls. Among them is the shape of the pool of tea in the bowl, which should be interesting, but in good taste. There are also various points concerning the base: It should have a pleasant roughness for the hands, but it must not be so uneven that the bowl will not stand steadily on the floor.

Two different glazes are used on Raku teabowls: one black and the other red, both thick and lustrous. These colors are considered to make the best contrast to the bright green of the powdered tea. The black Raku ranges in color from deep shiny black to a red brown; the red Raku is of a soft salmon red, sometimes with a little green or white in it. Both are low-fired lead glazes that are allowed to flow down the bowl unevenly.

In the tea set given to Mrs. Jack Gardner of Boston by Okakura Kakuzō (who was curator at the Museum of Fine Arts, Boston) there is a pottery badger incense case by Raku Kichibei (late eighteenth century), an ash dish by Raku Ryonyu IX, 1800, and a pottery teabowl "Black Peony" (Ill. 23) by Raku Seisai (early nineteenth century). (Famous teabowls were given names.) The teabowl in Ill. 54, made by the twelfth generation Raku Kichizaemon, was made with gray clay, with a brilliant black glaze having three large splashes of dull red. The maker of this bowl was mentioned by Edward Morse in his *Japan Day by Day*, as Morse visited him at his Kyoto home.

The present (fourteenth) Raku uses the same kilns that have been used since the time of the eleventh Raku. There are two of them, one for the black Raku and one for the red, the red being fired at a lower temperature than the black. Both kilns are in the backyard of the same house in Kyoto where the family has lived and worked since the time of the third Raku.

Teabowls can be found in various sizes and shapes. Large bowls were intended for thick pasty tea and smaller ones for thin foamy tea, and different teabowls have always been made for winter and summer use. Those made for winter are higher, with smaller openings, in order to conserve the heat of the tea; summer ones are wider so that there is more surface, to increase the cooling. The teabowl in Ill. 54 is a shallow summer one; in Mrs. Gardner's tea set (Ill. 23) both a summer and a winter one are shown.

54. Raku teabowl, made by Kichizaemon, twelfth generation, c. 1880. This teabowl (cha-wan) is shallow and curved to a small foot. It is of dark gray clay with brilliant black glaze having three large splashes of dull red.
Metropolitan Museum of Art, Gift of Howard Mansfield

55. *Vase* (shakutate) *of red Raku ware, Kyoto; twentieth century. This is the type used in the tea ceremony to hold the water ladle and the fire tongs.* Metropolitan Museum of Art, Macy Collection, Gift of Mrs. V. Everit Macy

56. *Raku ornament in the form of an old woman. Tokyo, 1875.* Victoria and Albert Museum

Since Raku wares have a crackled glaze and a soft porous body, they permit liquid to seep into the body of the ware. In the course of time, however, with much use, the pores close and the wares no longer leave a damp ring where they have stood. Many ornaments are made in Raku ware (Ill. 56).

Ninsei

Nonomura Seibei, known by the artist name of Ninsei, was a Kyoto potter. There seems to be considerable doubt about his exact birth date, but it is generally said that he was born and raised in Tamba and learned his potter's craft both there and in Seto. He moved to Kyoto during the first half of the seventeenth century, after the Tokugawa regime had become established at Edo, and founded a kiln on the western edge of the city. There he came under the patronage of the prince-abbot of the Ninna-ji, a large temple at Saga close by, and began to produce decorated wares with overglaze enamel designs.

Kakiemon, in Arita, had discovered the secret of decorating porcelain with overglaze enamels only a short while before, but the two artists favored entirely different styles. Ninsei's decoration was in the traditional style, covering the whole surface, but Kakiemon rarely covered more than one third to one half of the area, contrasting his decoration with the beauty of the glazed surface. Ninsei's work was greatly influenced by the lacquer wares, many of his pieces having a black glaze as background to the enameled designs (Ill. 18).

Ninsei established and worked at kilns in many parts of Japan, and in consequence a wide variety of wares are referred to as Ninsei-*yaki*, some being in faience and some in semiporcelain. His wares are famous for the closeness and lightness of the body, and for the regular closely crackled glazes that enabled the enamels to adhere.

His influence has been far reaching, imitations being made by master potters as well as by those less adept. Mokubei, Ninami, Dōhachi, Eiraku Hozen, and Eiraku Wazen all copied his works, but put their own seals on their wares.

Kenzan

Ogata Shinsei, known by the artist name of Kenzan, was a pupil and follower of Ninsei. Unlike Ninsei, who came from a humble family, Kenzan came from a family that had been wealthy and aristocratic for a long time; they had served the Ashikagas for seven generations. His father, a rich dry-goods merchant, was also a good painter and calligrapher, and Kenzan himself was a poet before he became a potter, and was famous for his calligraphy. Ninsei gave Kenzan a copy of his notes, now in the possession of the Yamato Bunkakan Museum, and Kenzan made a notation inside that he had rewritten them, as they were in the language of a country workman, full of slang and dialect.

Kenzan's brother Kōrin was a celebrated painter. Together the brothers pro-

duced a number of ceramic pieces (Ill. 57).

In contrast to Ninsei, Kenzan was essentially a great decorator and not a particularly skillful thrower; many of the pieces he decorated had been thrown by assistants. His wares are in a soft low-fired faience, similar to Raku, and he favored simple shapes that lent themselves well to his painting and calligraphy. His square dishes are famous. His decoration was free and bold, painted in outline or flat designs, with a gift for understatement.

As Kenzan had no son to succeed him, he adopted one of Ninsei's natural sons (Ihachi), who took the title of Kenzan II. In fact, the Kenzan title was transmitted from one potter to another in recognition of style and not through any blood relationship. The third and fourth Kenzans were self-appointed successors to the title. Miura Kenya made wares in the Kenzan style, but renounced the title, transmitting it to Ogata Shigekicki, who became Kenzan VI.

Miura Kenya (1821–1889) was born in Kyoto. He had his first kiln at Fukagawa, and later moved to Mukojima. About 1860 he settled at Asakusa, in the northern part of

57. Square dish, buff pottery, potted by Kenzan, painted by Kōrin, and signed by both. Design of Jurojin, God of Longevity, reading a scroll. Courtesy of the Brooklyn Museum, A. Augustus Healy Fund

58. Bowl made by Miura Kenya. Raku ware, covered with a dark green glaze decorated with large white flowers with yellow centers. Victoria and Albert Museum

Tokyo, where his kiln was so small that it could be used in his house.

Miura Kenya's pottery beads were very popular, and he was famous for his copies of wares made by Haritsu, a potter who lived at the end of the seventeenth century. Haritsu had learned pottery from Kenzan and decorative lacquer work from Korin. He combined both arts, inlaying pottery in lacquer pieces, and using lacquer work on Raku ware, ornamenting the latter with shapes of flowers, grass, insects, and so on (Ill. 58).

Ogata Shigekicki (Kenzan VI) is famous for being the teacher of Bernard Leach, an English potter, and Tomimoto Kenkichi, who together held the title of Kenzan VII.

At the time when Leach sought him out, Kenzan VI was an old man whose art and works had been pushed aside by the new commercialism. He lived in poverty in a little house in the northern slums of Tokyo. No one wanted to buy the traditional-style wares that he made, and like many others trained in the earlier age, he could not adapt his style to the new ways. However, Leach tells us, many pieces now in Western collections said to have been made by Kenzan I were in actual fact made by Kenzan VI, or his predecessor Miura Kenya.

Bernard Leach, like so many before him, went to Japan to teach Western methods and stayed to learn Eastern ways. Trained as an artist, he went to Japan in 1909 as a young man with the intention of giving art lessons. About two years after his arrival, he attended a sort of garden party in Tokyo, given at an artist friend's house, where the guests were invited to write or paint on unglazed pots provided for that purpose. The pots were subsequently fired in a portable kiln set up in the garden. Each guest was able to see his pot come out of the kiln and be set on tiles where the crackle began to form and the true colors of the decoration emerge. This kind of party has been considered a gentlemanly entertainment for a very long time.

As a direct result of this experience, Leach looked for a teacher to instruct him in the art, and found Ogata Kenzan, who agreed to build him a kiln and teach him the traditional recipes. Leach spent nine consecutive years in Japan, learning all that he could of the potter's art (Ill. 59). He also persuaded Tomimoto Kenkichi to study with him under the guidance of Kenzan VI. Leach and Tomimoto together held the rightful title of Kenzan VII, being the only pupils of Kenzan who legally mastered the art. Both Leach and Tomimoto began their careers as potters making Raku ware. Leach then turned his attention to making stoneware and found much inspiration in Korean pottery. On his return to England he began to make English slipware in the tradition of the seventeenth century. Tomimoto's work is discussed in Chapter 9.

59. *Four pieces by Bernard Leach: Stoneware jug, gray body; off-white stoneware glaze inside and out, then outside dipped again in rusty brown iron glaze. The porcelain bowl has a creamy glaze with blue gray underglaze around the rim and iron brushstrokes over the glaze. Porcelain bottle with green tea dust glaze; iron brushwork turns tea dust to rusty* kaki. *Mug has* black temmoku *glaze breaking to rust where it is thin.* Frank Stoke

Awata Wares

Of the two kinds of Kyoto wares known as Ninsei-*yaki*, those made in faience are called Awata ware and those made in porcelain are Kiyomizu ware (Ill. 60).

The Awata wares have a soft appearance, with a pale yellow finely crackled glaze. The body is a light yellowish gray. During the Meiji era flowers, birds, and landscapes were popular motifs, and lavish amounts of gold were used. The main enamel colors were emerald green, lavender, and blue, with red, white, and silver used sparingly.

In the 1880s there were twelve families of potters working at the Awata kilns, each having a kiln and employing workmen. The best known of these potters were Kinkozan Sobei, Taizan Yohei, and Bunzo Hozan (who were all descendants of the original potters), and Tanzan Seikai.

60. Water jug, kiyomizu ware, eighteenth century. Philadelphia Museum of Art, given by Marion E. Potts; Photograph by A. J. Wyatt

KINKOZAN

Kinkozan Sobei, who was active during the latter part of the nineteenth century and early in the twentieth, was the sixth generation of the Kagiya family. According to Brinkley, the first potter (called Kagiya To-kuemon) began work at Awata in 1693. On the other hand, Kato Tokuro says that the first potter was called Genemon Kobashi (the family calling themselves Kagi-ya) and that he established a kiln at Awataguchi between 1644 and 1647. However, both agree that the potter of the third generation, Kagiya Mohei (Brinkley) or Kibei (Kato), was appointed to the Tokugawa court and took the name of Kinkozan. The Kobayashi family called themselves Kinkozan from this time onward, and, fortunately, thereafter we have less confusion over their names.

Sobei made some porcelain as well as the faience for which he is better known. Assisted by a large staff of potters, he produced a vast amount of export wares, which are signed with the painted Kinkozan mark in red. The family continued until the eighth generation (Ill. 61).

TAIZAN

According to some authorities, the Taizan mark was first used during the seventeenth century, but others state that it does not appear until the early part of the eighteenth century.

The first generation was a potter named Tokuro, whose son Yohei succeeded him. He called himself Taizan Yohei, and the oldest son of each subsequent generation was

61. Bottle with cloisonné, Kinkozan, 1895. The mark reads Nihon Kyoto Kin-kō-zan zo. *Pair of Satsuma tea caddies.* Fogg Art Museum, Gift of William H. Fogg

named Taizan Yohei. The family continued as far as the ninth generation; the kiln was closed in 1894. The wares are skilfully decorated, and the body is of a good quality (Ill. 62).

HOZAN

The first Bunzo Hozan came to Awata from Omi early in the seventeenth century, and his descendants continued there as potters for several generations. Morse commented on the originality, diversity, and beauty of the wares bearing the Hozan mark, and said that in those respects they exceeded all other Awata pottery (Ill. 63).

TANZAN

Tanzan Seikai was originally educated for the medical profession. He settled in Awata during the early 1850s, but did not assume his art name until 1869. Kato Tokuro says that when Prince Shoreiin established a pottery exchange in 1853, he ordered Tanzan to produce Awata pottery.

Tanzan had two sons, Yoshitaro and Matsuro, both of whom succeeded him at the kiln. Tanzan made porcelain as well as pottery, and produced many showy pieces for the export trade (Ill. 64).

Kiyomizu Wares

We are told in Augustus Franks's *Japanese Pottery* (1880) that the Kiyomizu factory was started by Otowaya Kurobei and others who came from Seikanji-mura, in the Horeki Period (1751–1763). Franks says:

In the beginning of the present (18th) century, Takahashi Dōhachi, Waké Kitei, and Midsukoshi Yosobei commenced to make Sometsuké, or porcelain decorated with cobalt underneath the glaze, in imitation of Arita ware, from clay imported from Idsumi-yama, in Arita, in the province of Hizen. Most of the productions were shaped by hand, and in such good taste that they have grown into favour with drinkers of tea or saké. The factories have since de-

63. *Fire bowl, marked Hozan; nineteenth-century Awata ware, Kyoto.* Metropolitan Museum of Art, gift of Mr. and Mrs. Samuel Colman

64. *Pair of vases by Tanzan, Kyoto; nineteenth century.* Metropolitan Museum of Art, Gift of Charles Stewart Smith

veloped and increased in number, and there are now eleven families of porcelain makers, of whom the more prominent are— *Kanzan Denshichi, Muruya Sahei, and Kameya Bunpei; and twenty-one families of faience, notably Takahashi Dōhachi (second generation), Waké Kitei (second generation), Kiyomidzu Kichibei, Kiyomidzu Rokubei, Seifù Yohei, and Mashimidsu Zoruku. Each family has its own factory independent of others, but rarely in common. The total number of factories in this district is twenty-one. Each is formed of six or seven kilns ranged side by side. The produce consists chiefly of tea and saké utensils, and occasionally of ornamental objects, such as flower vases or incense burners. They mostly belong to the Sometsuké class, but recently different coloured enamels have been used for their decoration. The latter, however, is not equal to the former, with the exception of the work of Kanzan Denshichi, who decorated with gold on red ground, in imitation of Yeiraku; and has also invented a manner of representing, in porcelain, iron inlaid with gold.*

DŌHACHI

The first Dōhachi (1737–1804) was the second son of Hachiro Takahasi, a samurai from Isé. He came to Kyoto as a young man and opened a chinaware shop. Later, he studied with Eisen and established a kiln at Awata. Ninami Dōhachi, the second of the line, the son of the first Dōhachi, also studied with Eisen. He was celebrated for porcelains decorated in Chinese-style blue and white and for pottery in the Ninsei and Kenzan style. He died about 1856.

Franks speaks of the Dōhachi at Kiyomizu in the 1880s as being the second generation, but in this he is not correct. No doubt the confusion arose because the third and fourth generations used the same marks as the second, and, as with other dynasties of potters, the works of one generation are often hard to distinguish from those of another, especially when the same seals are used.

Dōhachi III, the son of Ninami, worked at Momoyama but moved to Satsuma about 1850; he went later to Arita. His blue and white pieces are famous, particularly those

65. Bowl by Dōhachi, Kyoto; nineteenth-century Kiyomizu ware. Metropolitan Museum of Art, Gift of Mr. and Mrs. Samuel Colman

66. Dish and vase, made by Seifu III (1851–1914), Kyoto; nineteenth century. Courtesy, Museum of Fine Arts, Boston; Hoyt Collection

decorated with clouds and crows. He died in 1879, and his son, Dōhachi IV, died in 1897. Dōhachi V became president of the Kyoto Potters Association; he died in 1915. Dōhachi VI is still living.

SEIFŪ

The first potter of this line was called Seifū Yohei (1806–1863); his art name was Baihei. The son of a bookseller in Kanajawa, he went to Kyoto in 1844 and studied ceramics under Ninami Dōhachi. His kiln, where he made porcelain and some faience, was at Goyobashi.

Seifū II, called Gohei, made only porcelain. Seifū III (1851–1914) adopted all the new methods of the day, and is particularly famous for his white pieces decorated in low relief with flower and plant designs (Ill. 66). He also made celadon wares and pieces decorated with underglaze red. Wares made by the three Seifūs are so similar that it is often difficult to differentiate between them.

KITEI

This family made blue and white porcelain wares for seven generations at Gojosake, as well as pottery in the Dōhachi style. The third generation is said to have worked with Rokubei.

ROKUBEI

Rokubei I made finely decorated faience, blue and white wares, and also black Raku, for which he received the art name of Rokubei from Prince Myoin. He was the son of a farmer in Setsu Province who came

to Kyoto and built a kiln at Gojozaka with Waké Kitei in the second half of the eighteenth century. Seisai, the son of Rokubei I, became Rokubei II, and besides making similar wares to those produced by his father, was noted for his blue and white porcelain in the Chinese style and his wares with monochrome glazes. He died in 1847, according to Morse, or 1860, according to Brinkley. Rokubei III, known as Shoun, was famous for his earthenware teapots with enameled decorations of crabs. He also made a large garden lamp in blue and white porcelain, which has been in the grounds of the

67. Porcelain wine pot with polychrome enamel decoration, by Kitei, Kyoto. Late nineteenth century. Metropolitan Museum of Art, Gift of Mrs. V. Everit Macy

68. *Late nineteenth-century pottery dish, probably Kyoto, has imprinted blue underglaze design with red brown edge. Greenish glaze, Japanese character* fuku *(good fortune) on underside.*

Imperial Palace since 1853. Rokubei IV, Shorin, died in 1920; Rokubei V is still working in Awata. The wares of the different generations are hard to tell apart as they are similar and bear the same seals.

RENGETSU

A Kyoto potter famous for her individual style was the nun Otagaki Rengetsu. Her father was a nobleman of Isé, and she married at an early age. Unfortunately, both her husband and her only child died, and so she went into a monastery in 1823 at the age of thirty-two. There she made unglazed pots, mostly little teapots, without enamels. She modeled leaves and lotus flowers in relief on these wares, and decorated them with her poems.

A wide variety of anonymous pottery and porcelain wares made in Kyoto since the Meiji Restoration (1868) is generally referred to as Kiyomizu ware. Some pieces are decorated with a monochrome glaze, some have a polychrome enamel decoration, and others have blue and white designs on them (Ill. 68). Anonymous wares made in Kyoto prior to 1868 are generally called Kyō-*yaki*, or Kyō ware. If a piece appears to have had its enamel decoration applied by a printing or stamping device, it was almost certainly made after 1868.

Eiraku

The Zengoro family is another line of potters associated with Kyoto. The family

69. *Pottery washer for wine cups, by Zengoro Hozen, Kyoto; nineteenth-century.* Metropolitan Museum of Art, Gift of Charles Stewart Smith

name is Nishimura but Zengoro is the familiar name of these potters.

The first Zengoro was a native of Nara, where he died in 1558; his birth date is unknown. He made articles of unglazed earthenware, and is specially known for his earthenware *furo*, which are braziers used in the tea ceremony for holding charcoal fire. These particular braziers are known as Nara *furo*.

The second and third Zengoros continued to make these *furo*. The third Zengoro moved to Kyoto, where he received recognition from the tea master Kobori Enshū, who gave him a copper seal, which has also been used by the succeeding generations on their *furo*.

The family continued generation by generation to make *furo* in Kyoto. The tenth generation, called Zengoro Ryozen, received a seal from the tea master Sen-no-Ryosai as a mark of approval for his *furo*. He made other pottery wares for the tea ceremony too, as well as copies of Cochin chinaware, or *kōchi yaki*, which is a type of pottery decorated in green, yellow, and aubergine glazes, applied in broad washes of color separated by fine lines of molding. He died in 1841; his son, Zengoro Hozen, carried on the making of *furo*.

Hozen (1795–1854), the eleventh generation of the Zengoro family, made a wide variety of wares, both pottery and porcelain, besides the *furo*. Like his father he made

copies of Kōchi-*yaki* (Ill. 69), and he also made *sometsuke*, celadons, and wares in the Korean tradition. However, he is best known for his *kinrande* porcelain (with scarlet and gold decoration in brocade style) and his *akaji-kinga* (gold designs on a red background).

Hozen was given two seals, one gold and one silver, by Lord Harutomi of Kishu.

70. *Porcelain bottle for sweets, by Zengoro Hozen, Kyoto; nineteenth century.* Metropolitan Museum of Art, Gift of Charles Stewart Smith

71. *Pottery teabowl made by Zengoro Wazen.* Metropolitan Museum of Art, Gift of Mr. and Mrs. Samuel Colman

One seal had the name Eiraku on it; the other, Kahei Shirui. Eiraku is the Japanese pronunciation of the Chinese ideographs forming the name of the Ming Emperor Yung Lo (1403–1424), in whose reign this red and gold type of ware was first produced. The name Eiraku has been used by succeeding generations in addition to their individual artist names.

The next two generations of the Zengoro line were both sons of Hozen. The elder, Wazen, was the twelfth generation; the younger, Zenshiro, became Zengoro XIII.

In his early years Wazen (1823–1896) helped his father. They made Koto ware at Hakone, Omi, on the shores of Lake Biwa, Koto meaning "east of the lake." Koto ware is a hard porcelain decorated in underglaze blue and overglaze enamels in Chinese *wu ts'ai* style. The kiln closed in 1860.

Like his father and Dōhachi, Wazen also made bowls with designs of maple leaves and cherry blossoms, the tree trunks on the outside of the bowl and the blossoms inside.

After leaving Hakone, Wazen built a kiln in the garden of the Ninna Temple in Kyoto. While there he made tea ceremony wares for the Princess Kazu when she was married to the shogun.

Wazen's most important work was done in Kaga, where his influence still remains. He went there in 1866 on the invitation of the Lord Maeda and stayed for five years. The porcelain wares he made there are known as Kaga Eiraku; they combine underglaze blue and white (*sometsuke*) with gold designs on a red background (*akaji-kinga*). He also perfected the Kaga *aka-e* style, or red decorations on a white ground.

After leaving Kaga, Wazen went to Okazaki in Mikawa, where he stayed for three years. About 1875 he moved to Higashi-yama, but he was in poor health and finally, in 1897, he died. He had no children, although he adopted a son called Sozaburo, who made very little ceramics and did not succeed to the title.

Kyokuzen and Toho were two different artist names used by Hozen's younger son Zenshiro. Apart from this, however, not much is known about him. Another potter is also often called the thirteenth Eiraku. This was Yasuke, who had been a pupil of Hozen and worked in a style very similar to his master's.

Tokuzen (1854–1910) was the fourteenth of the Zengoro line, but this generation is considered to extend to 1928, as Tokuzen's widow, Myozen, continued the work. Tokuzen worked in the family tradition and made some fine pieces. Two examples of his wares were shown in the 1876 Philadelphia Centennial Exposition. One was a pair of porcelain flower vases, decorated in gold on a red ground, with phoenixes among formal scrolls on the body and geometrical designs on the neck and foot. The other was a pair of porcelain sake cups with a celadon glaze on the outside and a gilt border.

Myozen, Tokuzen's widow, was an excellent potter. She was given a seal by Takamune Mitsui in 1912, and at the end of her life she used her name, Myozen, to mark her wares.

Shozen, a nephew of Tokuzen, became the fifteenth Zengoro. His succession to the family title was short-lived as he died in 1933.

Hozan, the sixteenth of the line, is at present living and working in Kyoto. He is variously known as Eiraku, Nishimura Zengoro, or Hozan. Besides following the traditional styles of his family, he also makes wares in his own individual style. His workmanship is excellent. The wares are made of a very thin hard porcelain, and the beautiful decoration reflects a modern trend.

7

Kutani

The small village of Kutani lies in the mountains of Kaga Province, near the northwest coast of Japan. It is a lonely place, cut off by mountains on one side from Kyoto and on the other side from the coast. The old way to Kutani was up the Daishoji River by boat. The name Kutani means nine valleys, and is descriptive of this mountain village. The feudal lords of Kaga were members of the Maeda family, which at the beginning of the seventeenth century was among the wealthiest clans in the country, its lands producing vast quantities of rice.

The history of the kiln at Kutani is wrapped in mystery. Records are lacking, and there is much disagreement about dates and even the kiln sites. One version is that in 1639 Maeda Toshiharu, whose mother was the daughter of the Shogun Hidetada, was given the rich rice-producing clan lands of Daishoji by his father. When porcelain stone was discovered at Kutani soon after this, a kiln was built by Tamura Gonzayemon, a retainer of Maeda Toshiharu, by his order. According to tradition, the kiln first produced tea ceremony wares, then blue and white wares.

It is generally believed that Maeda Toshiaki, Toshiharu's son, sent Goto Saijiro to learn the secrets of porcelain making and enameling from Kakiemon in Arita, as mentioned earlier. Goto Saijiro had previously been connected with a gold mine near Kutani. It was no easy task to gain the confidence of Kakiemon, so first he entered the kiln as a servant. Eventually he married Kakiemon's daughter, whom he deserted when he returned to Kutani in 1661.

Some accounts say that, before returning to Kutani, Goto Saijiro went to Nagasaki, where he met Chinese potters whom he took back with him; other accounts say that he visited China and brought Chinese potters back with him. Because of the lack of records, what really happened is a matter for conjecture.

The Kutani kiln closed down around the end of the century, the exact date being disputed. Why it closed is also a mystery, but it is believed to have been because of pressure from the shogunate.

The Maeda family was one of the "outside clans," not deeply attached to the shogunate, and since it was enormously wealthy, it was thus always a potential danger to the shogunate. Any traffic with China was an infringement of the laws of the shogunate, and if Goto Saijiro had gone to China, or brought Chinese potters to Kutani, this would have been enough to warrant his execution. Even a visit to Arita would have been a forbidden excursion.

At some time in the early 1690s the kiln was shut down and all the records destroyed. Goto Saijiro was summarily arrested and led away in chains to be executed. He swore to avenge himself after his death on the house of Maeda. This threat of ghostly vengeance must have had the desired effect on Toshiaki, as a substitute was found to be executed in Saijiro's place. (There is an old Japanese belief that if a man's mind is set

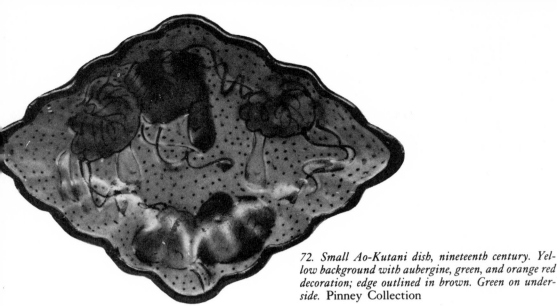

on vengeance at the moment of his death, his spirit will be able to carry it out.) One wonders about the feelings of the substitute, but history has nothing to say on the subject. Saijiro retired to the Jitsusein Temple in Daishoji and died there at the age of seventy in 1704.

Enameled wares of this period are called Ko-Kutani, or old Kutani. Some of them are so similar to Imari wares of the same period that it is purely a matter of opinion where they originated.

Ko-Kutani wares have more variety in the composition of the paste for the body than wares from any other kiln in Japan. The body is generally grayish white, coarse in quality, ranging from stoneware to porcelain. This variety would seem to indicate products from a number of kilns, and it has been suggested that the ships taking rice from Kaga to Hizen returned with undecorated porcelain from Arita as ballast, and that this porcelain was then decorated in Kutani.

The decoration of Ko-Kutani wares has a vigor unequaled by other kilns; it appears to have been originated by artists rather than craftsmen. The enamels are a vivid green, aubergine, Prussian blue, yellow, and a red ranging from cherry to brown; these colors, as well as the brushes used for the decoration, are thought to have come from China. Birds, flowers, and landscapes, as well as decorations of medallions and diapers, are painted in a bold free style. These pieces are either unmarked or have the Chinese ideograph *fuku* in a square.

In the Kutani group is a smaller one called Ao-Kutani, or green Kutani, much of which is made of stoneware. The enamels on these pieces are mainly green, yellow, aubergine, and Prussian blue, applied in broad washes and decorated with strong black lines (Ill. 72).

Nineteenth-Century Kutani Revivals

There were a number of Kutani revivals during the nineteenth century, some

73. *Figure of a girl playing the samisen (one of a group of four). Porcelain, 1870, Kaga.* Metropolitan Museum of Art, Macy Collection, Gift of Mrs. V. Everit Macy

74. Left: *covered jar, red Kaga ware.* Center: *Ao-Kutani flower vase with landscape; mark* fuku *(painted black on green).* Right: *Kutani teapot.* Peabody Museum of Salem; Photograph by M. W. Sexton

quite short-lived. The kilns were at various sites, mostly a short distance from the village of Kutani itself. We need not concern ourselves with most of them; they did not continue production beyond the middle of the century (Ill. 73).

Near the beginning of the nineteenth century (the exact date is uncertain), the Yoshidaya revival took place on the site of the old Kutani kilns under Yoshidaya Denyemon, a rich Daishoji merchant. The kiln was transferred to Yamashiro in 1814 under the supervision of Miyamoto Uyemon. The wares produced—called Saiko Kutani or revived Kutani—are credited with being the first to be stamped with a seal "Kutani."

Miyamoto Uyemon's son, Riyemon, succeeded his father in 1840, and about that time also Iida Hachiroyemon came to the kiln. Hachiroyemon was responsible for introducing a new style of red and gold porcelain ware. The richly decorated pieces with elaborate gold designs painted on a red enamel background are known as *akaji-kinga;* they are called red Kutani by foreigners (Ill. 74).

After Hachiroyemon's death in 1849, two sons of Hozen came to the kiln, and one of them, Zengoro Wazen, stayed for six years. Wazen was the twelfth generation of the family of potters known as Eiraku (see Chapter 6).

Wazen worked in the *akaji-kinga* style, and also brought to perfection the Kaga *aka-e* style, or red designs on a white ground. Many of his pieces have a red ground with gold designs on the outside and a white ground with red designs on the inside. Other pieces have red and gold on the outside and underglaze blue and white on the inside. Both these combinations are known as *hachiroye-yaki.*

These wares became so popular in Europe that kilns to make them sprang up throughout Kaga Province. Many bore the Kutani mark, and some pieces have the potter's signature incised in the biscuit.

The kilns went into a decline at the beginning of the Meiji era, but within ten years production increased, and since that time the kilns have been working steadily. All kinds of pieces are made: bowls, plates, dishes,

75. Porcelain censer, Kutani, 1870. Metropolitan Museum of Art, Macy Collection, Gift of Mrs. V. Everit Macy

76. Modern wheel-turned sake bottle, with Kutani mark. Gray body has shrimp and pine branch design. Pinney Collection. *Two sake cups, with Kutani mark.*

77. *Covered box has Kutani mark in gold on a red brushstroke. The porcelain is of good quality with considerable decorative detail; the European-style enamel decoration is not symmetrical but shows Japanese-style irregularity*

78. *This cup, saucer, and bowl bear the Kutani seal mark and "Made in Japan." Each of the six poets (five men and one woman) is portrayed with one of his poems. The painting of the tenth-century poet Ki no Tsurayuki suggests a source for the decoration on the Kutani pieces. His poem reads: "The breeze is not chilly beneath the cherry tree whose blossoms are flying; yet behold, from the sky falls a strange snow"* (Museum of Fine Arts Bulletin, *February 1921). Courtesy, Museum of Fine Arts, Boston, William Sturgis Ross Fund*

79. *Modern tea set with Kutani mark and "Made in Japan." The design of cranes with outstretched wings appears against a beige background spotted with gold. Red border is decorated with gold lines. Good quality heavy white porcelain. The close-up of the cup shows the Kutani mark in gold on a red circle.*

vases, incense burners, small ornamental objects, chocolate sets, coffee sets, tea sets, and so on (Ills. 75, 76, 77, and 78). Some have only the mark Kutani (Ill. 79); others have the potter's name as well, generally in gold on a red brushstroke. Seals are also used.

Many pieces have a ground enamel color over the glaze, the whole surface being decorated (Ill. 80). The brushwork is generally very good on elaborate designs. The characteristic red and gold is much in evidence, the red ranging from an Indian red through a red brown, differing from the Imari red, which is more orange.

Kaga Redwares (Kaga aka-e). These wares have red designs on a white ground, with touches of gold, mostly Chinese figures and landscapes, which cover the entire surface. They sometimes have a comb design on the foot rim similar to that on Nabeshima wares, but otherwise they are hard to distinguish from Kutani wares. Kaga redwares are usually of a very poor quality porcelain, soft and gray. Quantities of these wares were sent "in the white" from other parts of Japan to Kaga for decoration.

80. *All these Kutani pieces are late nineteenth century. The cup and saucer have Satsuma-style decoration.* Pinney Collection. *On the teapot, sugar, and creamer the ladies in red appear against a pale green enamel background.*

8

Satsuma and Satsuma-Style Wares

Satsuma is the general term for wares made at the Chosa, Ryumonji, Tateno, and Naeshirogawa kilns in Kagoshima Prefecture, Kyushu. These kilns were all in the domain of the feudal lord of Satsuma. However, in the period we are studying, the designation Satsuma covers wares made in the village of Naeshirogawa in the province of Satsuma (Ill. 81), and Satsuma-style wares made in Kyoto (Ill. 82), on the island of Awaji, in Yokohama, and in Tokyo.

At the end of the sixteenth century Shimazu Yoshidiro, lord of Satsuma, returned from an attempted conquest of Korea, and brought with him twenty-two Korean potters and their families. These families settled in Kagoshima and Kushikino, but in 1601 they moved to Naeshirogawa, where there were good white clay materials. Here, after many experiments, they succeeded in producing the ware now known as Satsuma.

81. Jar and wine pot with cover—faience, Satsuma ware, c. 1870. Metropolitan Museum of Art, Macy Collection, Gift of Mrs. V. Everit Macy

82. *Pottery jar (Satsuma type), by Okumura, Kyoto; late nineteenth century.* Metropolitan Museum of Art, Gift of Charles Stewart Smith

In Franks's *Japanese Pottery*, which was published by the Victoria and Albert Museum, London, in 1880 in connection with the Japanese ceramic collection displayed first at the Philadelphia Exposition of 1876 and sent to London the following year, is this description of the kiln:

The kiln is built on the slope of a hill, after the Corean system, and is of peculiar construction, differing from that in Arita and other places. It is built single, and not in a line as in other factories. It has a length of 150 feet to 200 feet, and a height of 5 feet in the centre, of a vault-like form. At the lower end of the kiln is the furnace, or rather the place to commence the firing. The fuel, consisting of dried wood, is thrown directly into the kiln, the inside of which communicates with the outer air by means of an opening in the side wall. Saggars are not used, and in consequence of this and of the irregular distribution of heat throughout the kiln, great damage occurs to the ware. Of the many places to which the art of pottery making was introduced from Corea, this is the only one at which the true Corean kiln exists.

The report goes on to explain that up to the time of the Meiji Restoration the families were kept entirely separate from the Japanese population, and intermarriage was prohibited. This preserved to a considerable extent their language and customs. At the time of the report there were about 1,450 of these people, all engaged in pottery making.

In our parlance (in contrast with old Satsuma and what the Japanese call Satsuma), Satsuma ware is a light porous semi-porcelain with a soft cream-colored crackle glaze showing ivory brown undertints. The glaze is a compound of feldspathic materials and wood ash, the crackle being formed naturally when the piece is fired. The biscuit and the glaze do not "fit" exactly; the glaze shrinks more than the biscuit, and this causes fine cracks to appear in it.

This cream-colored crackled ware has two most desirable qualities. One is that

83. Satsuma vase (faience), decorated with poly-chrome enamels and gilded. Mark: a cherry blossom, impressed, and "Isoyaki" in black. Early twentieth century. Victoria and Albert Museum

84. Satsuma vase, late nineteenth century. Excellent quality porcelain and decoration, with fine creamy crackled glaze. The overglaze enamels are in red, blue, turquoise, white, gold, yellow, and pink, with blue and red enamel dots. Color is rubbed into the glaze in places to accentuate the crackle.

white enamels may be used for decoration; the other is that, on account of the crackle, the decorative enamels sink into the cracks, and no matter how heavily they are applied, they adhere closely to the glaze and will not flake off or peel (Color Plate 13). Very often on this type of Satsuma ware the crackle has had color rubbed into it to increase the decorative effect (Color Plate 4).

The decoration is often floral and elaborate, and the brushwork meticulously executed (Ill. 83). Raised enameling was a popular feature (Ill. 84). This type of ware had great appeal for people of the Victorian age, for the heavy ornate decoration was in keeping with the styles of that era. Many pieces were of enormous size. Huge vases were placed at the foot of a staircase or on either side of a fireplace, as they generally came in pairs. Since the disappearance of cheap household help and, in consequence, of large houses, the modern home provides few places to display such pieces properly. Very small objects, such as buttons, hatpins, and buckles, were also made. They are still being made today.

At the turn of the century a blue and white Satsuma ware was made for export.

85. Satsuma vase, c. 1930. Faience, with the neck roughly ornamented with a knife. Mr. and Mrs. Herbert Cohn

86. Satsuma plate. Excellent quality; the brushwork is very fine. Mark on underside reads "Satsuma" in hiragana. Pinney Collection

87. Satsuma pitcher. This is an interesting piece, with Japanese ladies instead of the usual Chinese figures in this type of design. The shape has an oriental appearance. Probably late nineteenth century. The mark on the underside reads "Satsuma" in katakana.

The underglaze designs are mostly of Chinese landscapes and large peony blossoms, and the gray glaze has a fine crackle. These wares, again usually large, are generally incense burners or ornamental bowls.

Another type of ware, also for export only, had human figures in raised designs: warriors, saints, geisha, as well as writhing dragons or hō-ō (phoenix). The body of this kind of ware is almost completely covered with decoration; hardly any of the crackled glaze is visible (Ills. 88 and 89). No figures were ever painted on old Satsuma; the Japanese preferred simple flower decorations and landscapes, sparingly applied.

Almost all these export wares, although

88. Satsuma bowl with warriors. The Satsuma crest (a cross in a circle) occurs twice on the border.

89. Small Satsuma vase. The color is similar to that of the vase in Color Plate 13.

known to foreigners as Satsuma ware, were manufactured in Kyoto, Awaji, Yokohama, Awata, and Tokyo. They are known under those names to the Japanese.

In *Japan Day by Day*, Morse described a visit to the potteries at Awata and of the conditions that prevailed there around 1880.

The entrance to the potteries was reserved and modest; and within we were greeted by the head of the family and tea and cakes were immediately offered us. It seems that members of the family alone are engaged on this work; from the little boy or girl to the old grandfather, whose feeble strength is utilized in some simple process of the work. The output is small, except in those potteries given up to making stuff for the foreign trade, known to the Japanese as Yokohama muke; that is for export, a contemptuous expression. In many cases outsiders are employed; boys often ten years old splashing on the decoration of flowers and butterflies, and the like; motives derived from their mythology, but in sickening profusion, so contrary to the exquisite reserve of the Japanese in the decoration of objects for their own use. Pre-vious to the demands of the foreigner the members of the immediate family were leisurely engaged in producing pottery reserved in form and decoration. Now the whole compound is given over to feverish activity of work, with every Tom, Dick and Harry and their children slapping it out by the gross.

An order is given by the agent for a hundred thousand cups and saucers. "Put in all the red and green you can" is the order as told me by the agent, and the haste and roughness of the work confirms the Japanese that they are dealing with a people whose tastes are barbaric.

Awaji

In 1831 Kashiu Mimpei, a native of the island, erected a kiln in the village of Iganomura on the island of Awaji, after he had found suitable clay materials there.

Mimpei and his son Sampei produced wares that were very acceptable to the export trade. These were of a delicate yellow tint, similar to Awata ware, the glaze being covered with a fine crackle. The decoration was carefully painted with more or less transparent enamels (Ill. 90). However, be-

90. Flower vase, made by Kashiu Sampei, Awaji.
Victoria and Albert Museum

sides this type of ware, Mimpei also made
wares with single-color glazes—yellow,
green, or brown red in Chinese style. These
wares are sometimes known as Mimpei-*yaki*.
For them he often used the mark of a Chinese period.

It is of interest to note that at the Philadelphia Exposition of 1876 a tea service by
Sampei was exhibited. This consisted of a
gourd-shaped teapot, sucrier and cover, milk
jug, and two cups and saucers, all European
shapes.

Yokohama

In 1869 two Yokohama merchants established a kiln at Munami Otamachi (Ōta)
near Yokohama for the purpose of manufacturing an imitation of Satsuma ware for export. The materials were to be brought from
the province of Satsuma. The Yokohama harbor had just been opened to foreign trade,
and wares in Satsuma style were proving
very popular in the West.

A Kiyomizu porcelain maker,
Miyakawa Kozan, living at Makuzu, was
producing Awata-style Satsuma ware in
Kyoto, and he and his son were brought to
the Ōta kiln. Kozan's chance of success
abroad came with the Philadelphia Exposition of 1876. He applied for permission to
show his work there, and as he was still
young and poor, money was advanced to
him. With this help he produced some very
creditable specimens for the exhibition (Ill.
91). In 1893 he sent a collection of one hundred pieces to the Columbian Exposition at

Chicago. Particularly notable were his
peach-bloom vases with dragon designs.

Kozan was made a member of the Imperial Academy of Tokyo in 1896. He continued to exhibit successfully at foreign
exhibitions, and sent a small group to the
Panama-Pacific International Exposition in
San Francisco in 1915. The catalog mentions
four of his vases: two with landscape designs,
one with dragon design, and one with peonies. Two incense burners are also mentioned, one decorated with a phoenix and
one with a pheasant design.

Tokyo

Much Satsuma-style ware was decorated in the immediate area of Tokyo when
that city had become a center of foreign
trade after 1868. These pieces were brought
from kilns in other districts "in the white"
and decorated and fired in muffle kilns in
Tokyo.

Muffle kilns were also set up for this
purpose near other centers of foreign trade
—for example, Yokohama, Osaka, Nagasaki
—and it is practically impossible to distinguish whether this type of export ware was
decorated in one place or another. Much of
it is unmarked, and the pieces that do carry
a mark give the name of a decorator or kiln
that is not traceable. There were a great
number of such kilns, and many of them
were in operation for only a short time.

*91. Vase and cover, Satsuma style, made at Ōta, by
Kozan, 1869.* Victoria and Albert Museum

92. *Three late nineteenth-century Makuzu porcelains: a vase, a covered jar, and a second vase more bulbous in shape, which is marked "Kozan."* Vase at top: Courtesy of The Brooklyn Muesum; *other pieces,* Metropolitan Museum of Art, Gift of Charles Stewart Smith

93. Pair of blue vases with Satsuma-style decoration.

9

Meiji Classical, Traditional, and Neo-Traditional Potters

Although the advent of the Meiji era, with its onrush of Western ideas, was a disaster to the potters working in the old traditions, there shortly emerged a new generation of potters born into the now-established Western influence. Overall, potters from the late nineteenth century up to the present day fall roughly into the following groups: those who looked back toward China and aimed for the classical perfection of those wares; those who worked in the traditional forms and neo-traditional forms; those who turned to the folk arts for inspiration; the Nitten group; and, last, the avant-garde group. However, the potters in all these groups were influenced to some extent by Western ideas and methods.

In the first group Itaya Hazan and Ishiguro Munemaro are considered the leaders of their generation of potters who worked in the classical style of the Chinese tradition.

Hazan, born in Tokyo in 1872, made wares combining oriental tradition and Western design in a highly compatible manner, creating a form of neoclassical style. He displayed a high degree of technical competence in all his work. Especially worthy of mention are his white porcelains; also his celadons, which are usually decorated with flowers or leaves in shallow relief. Hazan studied European enameling techniques also and succeeded in creating new colors.

He instructed a large number of students, many of whom in their turn became

able potters, and many more were influenced by his work, directly or indirectly. He formed a group of potters called Tōtō-kai (Eastern group) who looked to him for leadership.

Although Ishiguro Munemaro was born in Kyoto in 1893, some twenty years after Hazan, his work is more in the pure tradition of the Chinese potters than Hazan's, and it shows little perceptible Western influence. A noted collector of Chinese pottery and stoneware of the Han and Sung dynasties, Munemaro adopted a style derived entirely from Sung Dynasty wares, and the perfection his pieces display is almost that of the originals. His pieces are masterpieces in their own right, however, dignified and elegant in both form and decoration. His teabowls and larger bowls, both with *temmoku* glazes, display a high degree of skill; the glazes are richer and finer than any used by other potters of recent times.

Kato Hajime (1900–1968) born in Yokohama, belonged essentially to the group of potters working in the oriental style and combining with it modern styles and designs from the West. He was a versatile decorator who used many different styles. He made pieces decorated with both the Sung-style decorations called *uki-botan* and *shizumi-botan*. *Uki-botan*, "floating peony," is a technique whereby the background of a decoration is beveled with a knife, so that when glazed with celadon glaze, the decoration (flower, bird, or other

94. *Late nineteenth-century porcelain flower vase by Takemoto of Tokyo. White, faintly green body with flambé collar, in Chinese style.* Metropolitan Museum of Art, Gift of Charles Stewart Smith

motif) appears to float on the surface of the piece. *Shizumi-botan,* "sinking peony," is the opposite technique, with the pattern incised at a lower level than the background, so that when glazed with celadon glaze the motif appears to sink into the body of the piece.

Another form of decoration that Kato Hajime used is in the sprigged-on technique. To make this type, plastic clay is pressed into a mold and then stuck onto the surface of a leather-hard piece with slip.

Kato Hajime also produced fine pieces through his modern adaptation of the carved biscuit mold. This mold has the form of the inside of the bowl, and the decoration is incised in it. A slice of clay is pressed onto the mold and trimmed, and a foot is attached. When the piece is finished, the pattern—now, of course, raised—appears on the inside of the bowl.

Besides these techniques, he also was master of overglaze enamel decoration, and his gold designs on a pale green background are particularly beautiful. He did extensive research into the various glazes used on the old wares of Japan and China, and as professor of ceramics at the Tokyo University of Arts, exerted considerable influence on the younger generation of potters.

Uno Sataro, born in Kyoto in 1888, devoted much of his life to the ancient art of celadons, and is outstanding for his mastery in this field. His wares with underglaze red decoration are executed with consummate artistry. He also makes Chinese-style wares, but with a modern interpretation.

Takemoto Hayata, of Tokyo (1848–1892), must be included in this group, although he was born earlier than the others discussed in this section. He was a young man when the trend toward Westernism began, and received the full brunt of the new ideas during his most impressionable years. However, he was one of those who felt it was wrong to replace the ancient arts of Japan with worthless copies of Western fashions, and he determined to demonstrate the value of the old ways to the Western world (Ill. 94). He exhibited some of his wares at the Paris Exposition in 1878, but prepared a much larger collection for the Columbian Exposition in Chicago in 1893, where one hundred of his porcelains in solid colors were shown. Unfortunately, he did not live to see his success at that exhibition. The exhibition catalog reads:

> *These pieces are the fruit of ten years study and labor in the effort to revive the lost arts of China and Japan. These works are the last results of the artist's untiring and numberless experiments. They were made especially for the exhibition at the World's Columbian Exposition. The artist's over-exertion led to his untimely death. He died shortly after the last of these pieces were taken from the oven.*

The group of potters working in traditional and neo-traditional Japanese styles is a large one. The traditional group reproduce as faithfully as possible the traditional wares, but the neo-traditional potters work in a modern adaptation of the old forms, giving the traditional styles a fresh approach.

Sakaida Kakiemon of Arita (born 1906), the thirteenth generation of his family, works in the family tradition. His wares stand comparison with the best wares made by his ancestors.

Imaizumi Imaemon (born 1897), also of Arita and the thirteenth generation of his family, produces excellent quality wares using the old family designs. The Imaizumi family originally decorated the Nabeshima wares, but since the Meiji era they have

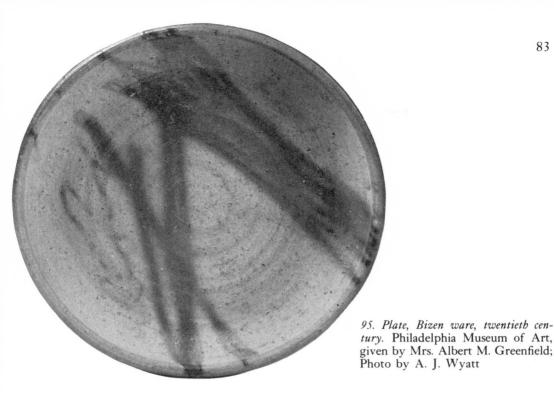

95. Plate, Bizen ware, twentieth century. Philadelphia Museum of Art, given by Mrs. Albert M. Greenfield; Photo by A. J. Wyatt

made the biscuit as well. At the present time their wares are technically almost equal to the old wares. Imaizumi Yoshinori (born 1926) also works in the family tradition.

Both Sakaida Kakiemon and Imaizumi Imaemon have been designated *ningen kokuho,* "living national treasure."

Arkawa Toyozo, born in 1894, is a native of Tajime in Gifu Prefecture, the site of the Seto-Mino wares of the Momoyama Period, where Shino and Oribe wares were made. He studied pottery under Miyanaga Tozan of Kyoto, and assisted in the excavation of the old Shino kilns at Okaya. In 1957 he published an authoritative work on old Shino.

Famous for his Shino, Seto-guro, and Ki-Seto wares, Arakawa Toyozo is especially well known for a teabowl in the Shino style. Through careful experimentation he has produced some very successful pieces that are consciously distorted to a high degree. His wares are excellent in quality and almost impossible to tell from the old ones, although certain connoisseurs insist that they do not have the rugged strength of the originals. He uses a semiunderground type of *ana-gama* kiln, which he built himself in 1933; it is the only one of its kind in Japan today. He too is designated a "living national treasure."

A number of potters work in the tradition of the Six Ancient Kilns (Seto, Echizen, Tokoname, Bizen, Tamba, and Shigaraki), as well as other old kilns (Karatsu, Hagi, and so on).

Kaneshige Toyo, born in 1896, of Imbe, Okayama Prefecture, is noted for the faithfulness with which he produces his Bizen ware. He represents the seventy-eighth generation of Bizen potters who have been making pottery continuously for over a thousand years.

The quality of Bizen wares deteriorated greatly during the Meiji era, when the kilns were no longer under the protection of the daimyo. Western methods and ideas had been imported with disastrous results, and Kaneshige determined to improve the quality of this ware that had carried on over such a long period. He revived the traditional methods after considerable experimentation, as the old methods had been allowed to die out; it was only after much trial and error that he rediscovered the secrets of making the fine old ware. Armed with this knowledge, he encouraged the local potters to work again in the old trusted ways (Ill. 95).

The wares he produces are of comparable quality to the Ko-Bizen wares, but despite the time-honored approach, he manages to impart to them a modern touch, like a breath of fresh mountain air.

Kaneshige (modern Japanese potters are generally known by their family name) uses a clay that is not screened—only the large pieces of rock are removed. Many small pieces remain, and during the firing these pieces explode, producing "bumps" on the clay walls, surrounded by cracks radiating from the high spots. As the method of packing the kiln for firing is to stack long-necked pieces on their sides, the pieces are often distorted, a characteristic very attractive to the tea masters, as any natural deformation or change caused by the firing has always been.

Bizen wares are never artificially glazed, the only glaze, called *goma*, being the natural result of ash falling on the ware during firing. Kaneshige's Bizen tea ceremonial pieces with cross-flame effect are highly prized in Japan. His work has been seen by a wide public in the United States in the years immediately following World War II. He was one of the well-known Japanese potters who came to this country for lecture demonstrations and exhibitions of modern Japanese ceramic techniques.

Fujiwara Kei (born 1899) is another native of the district who produces Bizen ware; his is made in a similar style to that of Kaneshige Toyo. The subtle coloring of his glazes and his decorations, which are modern although in the traditional style, makes his wares most pleasing and acceptable. He has achieved some beautiful effects through his use of the traditional Bizen decoration called *hidasuki*. This ancient form of decoration is made by using straw rope that has been soaked in salt water, and wrapping it around the ware; during the firing, the straw is burned up and the ash causes streaks of bright red glaze to form on the otherwise unglazed ware. Fujiwara Ken (born 1924) and Fujiwara Yu (born 1932) also work in the Bizen style.

Asai Rakuzen works in the Tokoname tradition. Tokoname wares are famous for their Chinese-style red, unglazed burnished surfaces. Asai Rakuzen has experimented with the Bizen-style decoration *hidasuki*, but uses seaweed instead of rope to wrap around his leather-hard pots. The resulting red streaks of glaze are very effective on his beige-colored wares.

Kikuyama Taneo began his research into the ancient methods of the Iga tradition in 1937, when he built himself a three-chamber *nobori-gama* kiln. He fires his wares from ten to thirteen times each, and although his kiln holds about three hundred pieces, he may consider only five or ten of the finished pieces to be acceptable. This is on a good firing; on a poor firing there will be fewer.

The Nakazato family of Karatsu has a 360-year tradition as potters, and Toroemon (born 1923), the present head of the family, works in traditional style. Nakano Suemasa is another Karatsu potter.

A descendant of another old potter family, Miwa Kyuwa makes Hagi wares. He is the tenth generation of the Miwa family, the first, Miwa Kyusetsu, having settled at Hagi in the seventeenth century.

Miwa Kyuwa produces tea ceremony wares that show combined Korean and Japanese influences. He uses the local light soft clay, which, when mixed with some darker clay from Mishima and sand, acquires a faintly pinkish color. Although in earlier days he used creamy white glazes as well as pinkish ones, he now confines himself to a variety of white crackled glazes, composed of a mixture of feldspar, wood ash, and rice husk ash. The glaze is applied by dipping the wares in it—he never uses a brush—and the sole decoration consists of drips or runs of glaze. He uses a hundred-year-old climbing kiln, which he fires once or twice a year; the firing lasts forty hours, and the wares are left in the closed kiln for three days to cool.

Ito Tozan, Tozan III, is the last of the traditional Awata ware potters. Although the Kyoto clay used for this ware is no longer available, Tozan has managed to mix a blend of clays that, when fired, has a comparable appearance to the original clay, and the fine mesh crackle glaze also has the good qualities of the original glaze. The creamy body is tastefully decorated in overglaze enamels.

The Kato family has been making pottery in the Seto area ever since the thirteenth century. Because the family is so old and large, there is considerable confusion about the names and dates of its various members, especially as several potters had the same name.

In the beginning of the nineteenth cen-

96. An inscription on the porcelain cup and saucer reads "Made by Kato Gosuke, in the province of Mino, Japan." 1875. Victoria and Albert Museum. The covered porcelain pot, 1890, is by Kato Tomotaro. Metropolitan Museum of Art, Gift of Charles Stewart Smith

tury Kato Tamikichi spent four years studying porcelain making at Arita, where he married the daughter of a porcelain manufacturer established there. On his return to Seto he made *sometsuke* porcelain, using the local *gosu*. He died in 1824, and was succeeded by his nephew Tamikichi II, who continued to make fine porcelain. Kato

Gusuke also made fine porcelain and sent a collection to the Philadelphia Centennial Exposition of 1876 and to the Paris Exposition in 1878 (Ill. 96).

Kato Tokuro (born in 1898) is well known for his wares in Shino, Oribe, and Ki-Seto styles. Although they are highly traditional in spirit, they show some of the

Western influence he was subject to in his early years.

His son, Kato Mineo, besides working in traditional style, has experimented with modern methods and ideas and has produced some interesting work in a new style. He has made distinctive pieces with rope-impressed designs, in Jōmon style, stark and strong. To make these pieces he forms them first by coiling, then beats them with a paddle wrapped with rope until they have an angular appearance of extraordinary antiquity.

Kitade Tojiro was born in Kanazawa, the district noted for its Kutani ware. He received his early training in the Kutani technique, and to this he has brought a fresh outlook. His mature wares are noted for new designs enhanced by a master's touch of color and brush.

Kyoto potters of the new school who make wares in the Kyō-*yaki* tradition are Kusube Yaichi, Yamada Tetsu, Kiyomizu Rokubei, and Kondo Yuzo. The products of these four potters all retain the characteristics of the older ware, but all have a flavor of the new age.

Kusube Yaichi (born in 1897) is well known for a carved style of decoration, with graceful motifs closely copied from nature. He first outlines the decoration with a sharp knife, then carefully carves and models the details in low relief.

Yamada Tetsu (born in 1898) began to study pottery seriously at the age of thirty-four. At that time he was a Buddhist priest and had been master of a temple since he was twenty-two; he was also a skilled calligrapher. When he became established as a potter, he left the priesthood, and since then he has striven to create a new Japanese style of pottery. Famous in Japan for his teabowls, he decorates his wares with a combination of wax resist and superimposed glazes.

Kiyomizu Rokubei, the fifth generation of the Kyoto family of potters of that name, was born in 1901. His wares have a traditional rustic quality, rich in the strength and vigor of peasant wares. However, the rugged vitality of the structure of the wares looks toward the twentieth century rather than backward to preceding centuries.

Kondo Yuzo (born 1902) has made some very fine blue and white pieces, with the bold designs at once modern yet traditional in style. He also combines other colors under the glaze, in particular a red from a copper mineral. These pieces with their blue and red underglaze decoration on a white background are most effective. Another technique he has mastered with great success is inlaying two clays of different colors on the same piece (*zōgan*). He has made some beautiful floral decorations in this style, the flowers in one color, the leaves in another, against a natural clay background.

Here we must stop and look at the giant, the master of all the traditional styles, Kitaoji Rosanjin (1883–1959). He was born in Kitaoji, Kyoto, and given the name of Kitaoji Fusajiro. After a very unhappy early childhood in several foster homes, he was adopted by a wood-carver and seal engraver, Fukuda Takeizo, and his wife, and he remained with them and learned to use his adopted father's tools.

His first artistic ambition was to become a calligrapher, and at thirteen he applied for entrance to the Kyoto Municipal Art School, which rejected him. He then entered three examples of his calligraphy in a contest and won first, second, and third prizes, which provided him with enough money to support himself. Thereafter he continued to enter, and to win, contests. However, he wished to study under someone, and he applied to two great calligraphers, asking to become a pupil, but both rejected him. In Japan it is very hard to accomplish anything without a correct introduction, and as Rosanjin had no one to help him, he was rejected for this reason rather than for any lack of talent on his part. Nevertheless, he still persevered, and he called himself *"Doppo"* ("lone wolf").

In spite of the discouragement and difficulties he had suffered, he made a name for himself as calligrapher, signboard carver, and engraver of seals, all of which require considerable artistic ability in Japan. At the age of twenty-seven he took the art name of Fukuda Taikan (Fukuda was the name of his adopted father). Ten years later, around 1920, he changed his art name to Rokyo ("foolish lord"). He altered his name once more, and by 1925 he was calling himself Rosanjin ("foolish mountain person").

Rosanjin had two passions, one for collecting antiques and the other for food. When his antique collection became too large to be comfortably housed in his dwelling, he opened an antique store in Kyobashi, Tokyo. At times he served his customers with choice foods, and as his visitors returned time and again for more of his delicacies, in due course he opened the Bishoku Club on the second floor of his store, a gourmet paradise. Eventually Rosanjin felt it was necessary to have more suitable and specialized dishes on which to serve the food, commenting that dishes are the kimonos of good food.

This wish led him to open the Hoshigaoka kilns at Kita Kamakura, near his large farmhouse residence, and he brought together a number of the best potters to work there. Both Arakawa Toyozo and Kaneshige Toyo were closely associated with him. He was insistent that the right

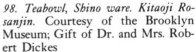

97. Teabowl with decoration of grasses is stoneware of the Bizen type. Kitaoji Rosanjin. Seattle Art Museum, Gift of Alice Boney

98. Teabowl, Shino ware. Kitaoji Rosanjin. Courtesy of the Brooklyn Museum; Gift of Dr. and Mrs. Robert Dickes

99. *Stoneware dish in the shape of a lotus leaf, brown glaze. Kitaoji Rosanjin.* Philadelphia Museum of Art; Purchased: The Far Eastern Revolving Fund; Photograph by A. J. Wyatt

100. *Chopping board* (manaita). *Kitaoji Rosanjin.* Philadelphia Museum of Art; Purchased: The Edgar V. Seeler Fund; Photograph by A. J. Wyatt

101. *Square platter with decoration of birds and grasses in underglaze iron; lower third of the surface is covered in copper green iron glaze; signed with incised katakana "ro." 12". Kitaoji Rosanjin.* Mr. and Mrs. Joseph Gordon; Photograph by O. E. Nelson

102. *Vase with pinched ears and decorative marks in iron brown; signed with incised characters.* Kitaoji Rosanjin. Anonymous loan; Photograph by O. E. Nelson

103. *Widemouth soy sauce pitcher with lid, spout, and loop handle attached at side, and overall translucent copper green glaze; signed with incised katakana "ro."* Kitaoji Rosanjin. Sidney Cardozo; Photograph by O. E. Nelson

104. *Small dish with design of crab in blue and brown underglaze, stylized star and ovoids, and red enamel rim on white porcelain body; signed with character "ro" in underglaze blue. D. 4 ⅞".* Kitaoji Rosanjin. Robert Ellsworth; Photograph by O. E. Nelson

105. *Bowl with decoration of grapes, vines, and leaves in underglaze iron brown of varying thicknesses as an opaque grayish overglaze, scorched light orange where thin; signed on the side with incised katakana "ro."* Kitaoji Rosanjin. Sidney B. Cardozo

106. *Plate D. 7". Delicate incised lines in the center portray tall grasses, heavy with grain, swaying in the wind. Kitaoji Rosanjin.* Captain and Mrs. Roger Gerry

clays be used, and he sent for whatever was needed from its original source, no matter how far away, even to Korea.

Rosanjin was always searching for new forms and ideas. When he found something that pleased him he would have it copied, and he was the first contemporary potter to have molds made for his use. He rarely made a piece entirely on his own; instead, he would supervise the making of the basic shape, and when it was finally formed to his satisfaction he would take it in his own hands to finish. It was from this point, however, that the piece took on individuality, as he subtly changed its form, squeezing it here, pulling it there, decorating it with a few brushstrokes, an incised design, or with various glazes. No matter in what style he worked, the finished piece was never a mere copy; it was always a Rosanjin, original in design and rich in aesthetic taste.

Although we have become used to the idea of an individual potter going through the whole process of making his wares on his own, forming them, then decorating them, this is a quite recent development in Japan. Such a task as throwing a piece on the wheel was considered menial work, suitable only for an artisan and completely unworthy of a potter's attention. It was only through the efforts of Bernard Leach and Tomimoto Kenkichi that this idea changed, and an artist-potter came to feel that every aspect of making a pot was part of his artistic creativity. Thus, when Rosanjin personally supervised the making of the basic form of his

wares, he was—according to normally accepted methods—actually paying a remarkable amount of attention to all stages of the process.

Perhaps the most remarkable facet of Rosanjin's genius was that he was able to work in so many styles: *sometsuke*, Chinese porcelains, Kutani, tea wares of the Momoyama Period (Shino, Oribe, yellow Seto, black Seto), Bizen, Shigaraki, Kenzan-style decoration, and so on. He also did a considerable amount of experimental potting, some of it in low-fired wares using various techniques of underglaze and overglaze decoration.

Rosanjin said that, although he had derived inspiration from the classic examples of the potter's art of both East and West, he always looked to the beauties of nature as his sole instructor, and always pursued the study of beauty. His pieces are essentially for use; a delight on their own, they are infinitely more beautiful when they are being used.

Although it was offered to him, Rosanjin never accepted the designation of "national living treasure." He had the self-sufficiency of a true artist who knew he stood apart, and so cared little for the opinion of his fellowman.

Tomimoto Kenkichi (1886–1963), the Kyoto potter, was born in Yamato Province (Nara Prefecture), and although he became Japan's first individual potter, he was originally trained in architecture and did not turn to pottery until he was nearly thirty.

When he was twenty-two he went to England to study architecture, and learned to speak English well. On his return to Japan three years later he met Bernard Leach, who had already spent a year there. Leach had come into contact with Japanese pottery and was anxious to study it himself, so Tomimoto, acting as interpreter, made arrangements for Leach to study under the guidance of Kenzan VI.

Leach tried to persuade Tomimoto to study pottery also, but Tomimoto returned instead to Yamato Province and continued his studies in architecture. However, he remained in almost daily contact with Leach, who wrote to ask for translations of terms that he did not understand. Leach finally managed to interest Tomimoto in studying pottery, and in 1915 Tomimoto built a small kiln for himself in Yamato, where he started to make Raku wares. He and Leach continued to exchange notes in their correspondence, and after a while they both came to the same conclusion: They should learn to throw wares on the wheel. This brought them derision and scorn from all sides, but they persisted and both learned to throw.

Tomimoto's early work was deeply influenced by Korean pottery, but although he worked in Raku and Awata style, he was not a *mingei* (folk art) potter and must be ranked as an important potter of the neoclassical school. He turned to Chinese-style porcelains after he abandoned the folk-art style, and decorated these pure white wares with elegant designs in cobalt. The refined original designs and sharp modeling are two important characteristics of his work. He was also an accomplished calligrapher and decorated his wares with beautiful calligraphic brushwork.

No doubt his greatest contribution to the art of pottery was his discovery of a satisfactory method to combine gold and silver in decorative designs (Ill. 108). Silver melts at a lower temperature than gold, and the old method was to fire first the gold, then the silver. Silver also tarnishes after a time, which is not desirable. After considerable experimentation Tomimoto discovered that if he mixed silver with platinum, it raised the melting point of silver, and permitted both the gold and silver decoration to be fired at the same time. The silver and

107. *Shallow dish, stoneware with a gray glaze and lotus painted in iron brown. Tomimoto Kenkichi. 1930–1935.* Victoria and Albert Museum

platinum combination did not tarnish, and the addition of platinum did not alter the color of the silver.

His enameled porcelains with decorations in red, green, gold, silver, and other colors are masterpieces of design, either when he adapts an overall pattern to fit the curved surface of one of his covered boxes or brushes a light airy pattern on a colored ground. A type of decoration in which he excelled was the combination of underglaze *gosu* with overglaze enamels. Pieces of this description are rarely made, since blue and white specialists do not generally work with overglaze colors.

Tomimoto worked hard to free Japanese pottery from the overpowering tradition of the *noren* family potters. As an individual potter, he realized to the full the difficulties of the young and struggling individual potter working outside a family tradition. In 1934 he instituted the ceramic section of the Nitten Academy, hoping that potters studying in this atmosphere would be able to realize their own individuality. However, after World War II he felt that the young potter at the Nitten Academy suffered too many restrictions to be able to develop satisfactorily into an individual artist, so he resigned from the academy and formed the Shinshō Craft Association (Shinshō-kai, New Craftsmen's Group) to help young potters and give them opportunities to exhibit their work. In 1949 he was asked by the government to found a ceramic department at the Kyoto Municipal College of Fine Arts; this was the first ceramic department established in any college in Japan.

108. Porcelain box with gold and silver designs. Tomimoto Kenkichi. Embassy of Japan, London

10

Folk Pottery and the Folk Art Movement

Japanese folk pottery is strictly utilitarian and crude, made of earthenware or stoneware in traditional shapes. It is a rugged ware intended for daily use, but it has a plain and functional beauty that is never ostentatious. The decoration, often in white slip, in simple and abstract designs, is usually combined with a poured or running glaze in a somber color—black, white, gray, dark brown, dark blue, or dark green.

The old oil dishes deserve special mention because—on account of their utilitarian, thick, heavy form—they had never been thought of as objects of aesthetic interest. But, with the awakening interest in the folk arts, their simple beauty became deeply appreciated, and their decoration has had considerable influence on craftsmen working in the movement.

Oil dishes *(aburazara* or *andonzara)* were made at Seto during the late Edo Period and the beginning of the Meiji Period (Ill. 109). They are flat dishes with a projecting rim, usually about seven inches in diameter; they were placed inside the lamp to catch oil dripping from the burning wick. The decorations are of remarkable beauty; usually they consist of just a few bold brush-strokes.

Very similar to these are the larger

109. Oil dish (aburazara or andonzara), *Seto.* Metropolitan Museum of Art, Howard Mansfield Collection

110. Porcelain plate, twentieth century. Courtesy of the Brooklyn Museum, Gift of David Jones

thicker plates (from ten to fifteen inches) that were also made at Seto of heavy stoneware. Used by peasants in their kitchens, they are known as *ishizara*. The decoration is similar to that on the oil dishes, free and bold with a minimum of strokes, and was either in iron black or the local cobalt found near Seto. Production of these wares ceased when cheaper mass-produced wares became generally available in the early Meiji era. Both these plates and the oil dishes are known as *getomono*, or ordinary wares.

Today folk pottery is made in many places throughout Japan. It ranges from traditional wares produced in the same places where they have been made for centuries to modern versions inspired by the traditional styles (Ill. 110). Traditional folk pottery has continued to be produced mostly in isolated and backward areas, where cheap porcelain is not easily obtainable. Kyushu, in the south, produces fine contemporary folk pottery, and there are several other areas that make these wares.

The kilns at both Ryumonji and Nae-shirogawa in Kyushu were founded by Koreans, and they continue to work in that tradition. At Ryumonji wares are decorated in a distinctive manner by swinging a dripping brush filled with slip over the ware; this produces a freely controlled pattern of lines and dots. Yanagi Sōetsu considered the wares decorated in this way with white slip over the dark Ryumonji clay body to be one of the distinctive *mingei* products of Japan. Similar effects are also produced with colored glazes over a white engobe. Another method of decoration unique to Ryumonji is *donko*, or superimposed glaze mottling, carried out in white and black glazes.

The Naeshirogawa kiln was originally founded for the purpose of making tea ceremony wares for the Lord Shimazu of Satsuma, who brought back Korean potters for this purpose on his return from Hideyoshi's Korean invasion. At first the kiln produced refined whitewares, but later turned to making black *temmoku* vessels for everyday use by the peasants of the area. The potters are still making wares with this beautiful black

111. Bottle, black Satsuma ware, made at Nae-shirogawa. Courtsey of the Brooklyn Museum, Gift of Frank L. Babbott

Satsuma glaze, which needs no decoration (Ill. 111).

The mountain villages of Koishibara and nearby Onda, also in Kyushu, have kilns operated by the local farmers, who combine pottery with their farmwork. In both villages the potters spend time morning and night, every day, on the preparation of their clay. In Koishibara, which was originally the parent kiln of Onda, there are twenty-five families in all, and nine of these are potter families who share two kilns. Each family owns two clay crushers, which work continuously day and night. The crusher is a pine log with a hammer on one end and a hollowed-out area on the other. Water is diverted from the local stream, and as it fills the hollowed-out portion of the log, it raises the hammer end; then, as the log is tipped up and the water empties out, the hammer falls onto the clay and crushes it. When the clay has been crushed well enough to satisfy the potter, it passes through a series of settling tanks; it is permitted to set in the last tank, and as the water evaporates, the clay is left in the form of a thick smooth mud. It is then put into drying bowls until it is of the right consistency to be placed in storage. The potters of Onda prepare their clay in the same way.

Onda potters had been making their wares for three centuries when Yanagi Sōetsu discovered the village and brought it out of its obscurity. Again, it too was a small settlement of a few farming families who fired their pots in the community kiln.

Wares made at Koishibara and Onda bear a great deal of similarity. Both are made by the old Korean method of first roughly coil-building large pieces on the wheel, then shaping them by throwing. They are decorated with *nagashi-gusuri*, "glaze that is made to flow," or superimposed glaze dripping; this is a process by which a contrasting glaze is allowed to drip from the top of a piece down the sides. Two contrasting glazes are frequently used.

A unique type of decoration is made by slip patting, and this technique has now spread to Mashiko, where the potters working in the folk art tradition use it with artistic effect. To make this decoration, the potter first centers the piece on the wheel. Then, while it turns slowly, he pats with a wide brush the liquid slip he has put in the center of the bowl. This forms a raised decoration of lines of slip radiating from the center of the bowl to the rim.

Kilns at both places use a sprigged-on decoration consisting of a raised motif stuck to the surface of the ware. This decoration has been used as a means of identification for a long time. The plum flower is the seal of Koishibara and the chrysanthemum the seal of Onda.

A very old traditional technique used at Koishibara is glaze throwing. The glaze is thrown either with a large brush, a small cup, or even by the handful. When a colored glaze is thrown on a white engobe, the result can be of unexpected beauty.

An interesting decoration used at Onda is called *tobi-kanna* or *kasuri-mon*, "chatter marks." This method originated in China during the Sung Dynasty, and although its use had died out in the country of origin, potters at Onda, in their isolation, have continued to use it. The name "chatter marks" is derived from the sound made by the flexible trimming tool as it jumps, or "chatters" on the surface of the ware. The dark body is first coated with a white slip; then it is put back again on the wheel, and the bouncing *kanna* held against the surface digs out small gouges, which show the brown body through the slip and result in a meshlike linear pattern that covers the whole body of the ware. This decoration is frequently used on lidded jars.

Wares made at Onda with a greenish blue glaze are particularly lovely, the beautiful cool color enhancing the quiet dignity of the simple shapes.

Other Kyushu folk kilns still in production are Futugawa, which has suffered a decline over recent years, Shiraishi, and Kuromuta.

In the main island of Honshu, the kiln at Tachikui in the Tamba district continues work in the traditional style of the area. Like Onda and Koishibara, Tamba in northern

Hyogo Prefecture owes its survival as a folk art producing center to its location in an isolated mountain region, although it is actually not situated at a great distance from the large cities. The local potters spend time morning and night preparing their clay, as at Onda and Koishibara; for them life has changed very little over the centuries. The wares they make are still in the simple straightforward shapes, and the usual decoration is a drip glaze over a contrasting color, white on black or brown, or vice versa.

Mashiko, fifty miles north of Tokyo, is a modern folk art producing center. Since Hamada settled there, at least thirty other potters have also arrived, and this village that has made folk pottery since early times has become the center of the modern folk art movement as far as pottery is concerned.

During the last century, wares made at Mashiko consisted mainly of water jars and salt pots with brown and persimmon glazes, as well as teapots with a "window picture" representing Lake Kasumi and Mount Tsukuba. This type of teapot is still being made. Wares known simply as Mashiko wares are made anonymously by the potters living there, and these utilitarian pieces show great taste and beauty, whether in the form of plates, cups, jars, or vases. They combine all that is good in the old tradition with an understanding of present-day needs, but nevertheless are not true folk art.

In northern Honshu the kiln at Naroaka in Akita Prefecture made use of a beautiful think bluish white iron glaze decoration. This glaze is called *namako-gusuri*, and when it is allowed to drip down over the glazed rough brown body the effect calls to mind an old Chinese poem by the Sung poet Lu Yu: "Fresh snow gleams on distant crags/Bathed in first glow of morning light." Unfortunately, this kiln ceased production after World War II.

Interesting folk wares still being produced in northern Japan are made at Hongo in Fukushima Prefecture. These traditional coarse peasant wares have been made for a very long time. The rough thick biscuit of a down-to-earth, unpretentious quality is

112. Cup, Hongo ware, a course peasant ware with thick rough biscuit. Private Collection

decorated with glazes in gray blue, dark brown, and deep green, highlighted with a bluish white *namako-gusuri* glaze (Ill. 112). The effect of these glazes on the dark pitted biscuit is of an exquisite lavender background to the free strokes of the contrasting glaze decoration.

The group of individual potters inspired by *mingei*, or folk art, and the awakened perception of the hidden beauty of those wares were mainly the result of the labors of Dr. Yanagi Sōetsu, considered by many to be a latter-day tea master in the tradition of the great ones of earlier centuries. Yanagi Sōetsu (1889–1961) deplored the passing of the traditional crafts of Japan and the way that they were being replaced by a worthless misunderstood copy of Western ways. Villages that in former times had produced beautiful pottery were now merely farming communities, the potters having returned to the land for their livelihood because their craft was no longer wanted. Up until the beginning of the Meiji era there had always been a ready market for their wares in their own villages or in markets in the area, but when cheap porcelain, mass-

produced by European methods, became available throughout the land, the coarse peasant wares were cast aside. Up to this time porcelain had been expensive, and only fairly affluent people had been able to afford it; the peasants had always used pottery or lacquer wares. With the new methods employed at Seto, Kyoto, and Arita, however, porcelain could be produced at a price that made it possible for even the peasants to buy it. Unfortunately, the people did not realize that they were replacing a priceless artistic heritage with cheap inferior products.

Yanagi Sōetsu was deeply distressed over the disappearance of the "unknown craftsman," steeped in a long tradition of hard repetitive work using methods evolved over centuries of trial and error by a patient humble people. Sōetsu's contention was that greater art has been produced by a people working together in such a way over a long period, in an abandonment of egocentricity and pride, than ever could be produced by one solitary artist, no matter how great.

Above all else, Yanagi Sōetsu prized the combination of beauty and usefulness: A pottery vessel should not only possess an abstract or aesthetic beauty, but also be of practical use. He felt that mere ownership of objects of value or those made by famous artists was no indication of a person's aesthetic taste. Rather, one's general surroundings and the objects used daily were the true criteria of taste.

Sōetsu gathered about him others who thought in the same way, notable among them Hamada Shōji and Kawai Kanjiro, and traveled throughout the country to visit potters in all areas and encourage them to take up their craft again. In 1931 Sōetsu, Hamada, and Kawai founded the Japan Folk Art Society (Nihon Mingei Kyokai), with the view of promoting interest throughout the country in the fast-vanishing folk arts.

In 1936 Sōetsu founded and became director of the National Folk Art Museum (Mingei Kwan) in Kokaba, Tokyo. This museum has a magnificent collection of crafts, and although it is primarily concerned with the crafts of Japan and Korea, it also includes those from China and other places abroad. However, besides the folkcrafts, it has work by the leading artist-craftsmen. In addition to the central museum there are now three provincial museums.

Yanagi Sōetsu also founded a magazine devoted to folkcrafts (kogei) and spent much of his time writing and making speeches. He awakened interest in Japanese folkcrafts in other countries; Bernard Leach in England and Langdon Warner in the United States have been active in promoting appreciation of Japanese folkcrafts in their countries.

The Japanese folk art movement now has over two thousand active and supporting members. About thirty groups of craftsmen are involved, and their wares are sent to the craft shops. The main folkcraft shops (Takumi and Izumi) are in Tokyo, but there are about fifteen others in other areas. Wares are gathered from all over Japan, and this helps to keep local handcrafts alive, encouraging them so that they do not vanish as mass production steadily grows. In fact, the movement has become a kind of substitute for the pre-Meiji protection of potters by their daimyos, which—although it tended to freeze the wares in traditional styles—also ensured the continued production of the wares.

Besides Japanese folk art, another source of inspiration for potters working in the folk art movement is Korean pottery of the Yi Dynasty. During this dynasty (1392–1912), Korea was invaded first by the Chinese under the Ming emperors and then by the Japanese under Hideyoshi in the sixteenth century. The resulting poverty and depression exerted a strong influence on the tastes and needs of the Korean people.

The ceramics of the period have a rather crude and primitive appearance. Nearly all the pieces were made of white clay with a glaze containing a small amount of iron, which produced a pale green on the white body. The wares seem to have been made quickly and almost carelessly, the glazes and slips being applied in a casual way; bowls are warped and have various other imperfections acquired during firing. The decorative brushwork seems free and spontaneous, whether it is in hakeme ("brush grain"), a decoration of swirling slip, or a painted design in underglaze red. These pieces have a simple beauty that has been unmatched in any other country or era.

Artist-potters working in the folk movement inspired by both the old Japanese folk wares and the pottery of the Yi Dynasty have originated a new type of ware, rich in simple beauty. These pieces are marked by their unpretentious style, which, although new, has an ageless quality and timeless appeal.

Hamada Shōji (born in Tokyo in 1894) originally trained as an engineer at the Tokyo Institute of Technology. Only after he began work at the prefectural ceramic research institute in Kyoto did he become interested in pottery. In 1920, curious about a teapot he had used as a child, he visited the pottery village of Mashiko, about fifty miles north of Tokyo, in Tochigi Prefecture, and saw potters working in the traditional ways. In the same year he became a student of Bernard Leach, went with him to England, and helped him start work at St. Ives. He stayed there for four years, and his style has been strongly influenced by the English slipware he saw while in that country. During this time in England he exhibited his wares in London in 1923.

On his return to Japan in 1924 Hamada Shōji settled in Mashiko, where he has re-

113. *Stoneware teabowl. Hamada Shōji.* Philadelphia Museum of Art, given by Mr. and Mrs. John F. Lewis; Photograph by A. J. Wyatt

115. *Stoneware jar, glazed in iron brown. Hamada Shōji.* Embassy of Japan, London

114. *Teabowl. Hamada Shōji.* Museum of Fine Arts, Boston, Hoyt Collection

116. *Dish of Karatsu-type ware. 12½″ square.
Hamada Shōji.* Philadelphia Museum of Art,
given by Mrs. Albert M. Greenfield; Photograph
by A. J. Wyatt

*117. Stoneware bottle, Hamada Shōji. H. 9″. Rich
warm brown covered with a semitransparent off-white
glaze.* William P. Semon, Jr.

118. Three pieces by Hamada Shōji. Plate, 9″: *rough
gray body with celadon glaze showing darker green
where brushed (perhaps with ocher) within the rim.*
Pitcher: *rough reddish buff body with milky off-white
feldspathic glaze with green brushwork (copper pigment) under the glaze.* Shallow dish: *rough gray
body, black* temmoku *glaze with trailed feldspar decoration.* Frank Stoke

mained ever since, steadily producing fine wares over the years. These wares have had a strong effect on contemporary studio pottery, not only in Japan but in the United States and Europe. In 1929 he held a one-man exhibition in the United States, and in the years following World War II he and other well-known Japanese potters came to the United States for lecture demonstrations and exhibitions.

Hamada works in high-fired stoneware, and prefers to make wares for ordinary use rather than for the tea ceremony. These wares include dishes, plates, bowls, teapots, teabowls, cups, bottles, jars, and flower vases. He works with freedom and ease in a relaxed manner, and throws boldly and fast. The resulting forms are strong, simple, and full of vitality, like peasant wares. His pots are rarely perfectly centered; he is satisfied if the piece is aesthetically pleasing and functions well.

He has a special technique for making large vessels. First, he throws the lower part normally; then, when this has become half hardened, he finishes the upper portion by coiling. This is the opposite of the old Korean method still in use at Koishibara and Ondo, where the lower portion is coil built. In contrast to the smooth curves of the Grecian style, his wares seem almost jointed, and we can sense Hamada's honest workmanship in the vigor of their construction. He makes use of molds to hand-press slabs of stoneware into square bottle forms. All his work is marked by a frank acceptance of the effects produced by a simple and direct approach. The clay he favors is soft and sandy with a high proportion of siliceous grit, which, when fired, gives a broken beady texture to the body of the ware.

Hamada's style is a combination of Japanese folk pottery, Korean pottery of the Yi Dynasty, and English slipware, used in an essentially practical way, modern and traditional at the same time. Like the traditional potter, he appreciates the characteristics of his materials, and uses one to enhance the other. The rough texture of the stoneware body provides an excellent contrast to both the heavy wood-ash glazes and the milky semiopaque feldspar glazes he uses; both body and glaze are shown off to their advantage by decoration in the soft warm colors he likes. His work illustrates in an intensely practical way the ideals set forth by Yanagi Sōetsu, how the ancient traditions may be applied to a modern world in a most acceptable form. Besides being an artist, Hamada is also a great craftsman.

The colors Hamada prefers are a rich brown, olive green, iron red, gray, and black. His designs are restrained and subtle. He makes frequent use of drip painting, letting the glaze drip from his brush apparently at random. He has also achieved new textures and color tones by his salt-glazing technique.

His effects are never contrived; a characteristic of Hamada's work is that he recognizes a spontaneous effect in each of his pieces and brings it out. This may be either in the form itself, a natural irregularity in the glaze, or perhaps a mood suggested by the decoration.

Hamada never signs his wares, although he signs the lids of the boxes collectors keep their pieces in. He feels that a piece should stand on its own merits and not need a signature. He once remarked: "Someday, the best pieces will be attributed to me, and those less good to my students." In 1955 Hamada was honored by the Japanese government with the Order of Living National Treasure, but far more important than that is the worldwide influence his work has exerted on contemporary pottery and will continue to exert during the years to come.

Sakuma Totaro has been a friend of Hamada for many years. He was never one of Hamada's students, but through a close association he has been influenced by Hamada's work. He has done many interesting things with glazes. Besides designs employing heavy applications of glazes (Ill. 119), he uses his own individual methods for dripping, trailing, and throwing them. Glaze throwing is a difficult technique but Sakuma has mastered it, and pieces with this form of decoration present a rich effect.

Sakuma frequently makes a type of inlaylike decoration called *mishima*, which is actually an impressed pattern with the raised areas standing out in a contrasting colored slip. This should not be confused with *zōgan* ("inlay"), which is a decoration made by strips of contrasting slip inlaid in a carved surface. Sakuma uses a clay roller stamp,

119. Stoneware bottle, Sakuma Totaro. Persimmon design in heavy glaze against neutral beige background; leaves of burnt umber. H. 9". William P. Semon, Jr.

120. Vase with mishima *(inlay) decoration by Shimaoka Tatsuzō. The piece has been flattened on four sides with wooden paddles; the glazes are earth tones. H. 9½". William P. Semon, Jr.*

which he carves into complex patterns, for his *mishima*. To counteract too much regularity, after the raised area has been decorated and the piece fired, he splashes a glaze over the entire object so that irregular trails of glaze drip down over the design.

Shimaoka Tatsuzō of Mashiko is one of the leading contemporary Japanese potters who works in Jōmon style using rope decoration. In his early days he studied with Hamada and, under his direction, made copies of Jōmon wares, which were being excavated at that time in the vicinity of Mashiko.

He also makes a *mishima* decoration, but unlike Sakuma's, it is the impressed area of the decoration that is in the contrasting color (Ill. 120). He has two different ways of making the pattern. One way is by rolling short lengths of wet heavy cord over the leather-hard surface to impress the design. The other way is with short lengths of bamboo around which cord has been wrapped and tied in various patterns; the bamboo is used in the same way as the wet cord. When the impressed pattern is completed, he paints over the patterned surface with contrasting slip, and when this is partly dry he scrapes it off the raised areas, leaving the impressed

areas in a contrasting color to the rest.

Another type of *mishima* decoration he uses consists of a stamped impressed design (Ill. 121), and is often combined with free carved lines. Both the stamped and carved designs are filled with a contrasting colored slip, making the pattern stand out in two-color relief.

Some of Shimaoka's wares feature *goma*, "sesame seed," iron spot decoration. These black or brown iron spots look like sesame seeds in the clay; they make their appearance when the piece is being fired and the glaze dissolves the iron in the clay. This decoration occurs naturally with the local clay of Mashiko, which is rich in iron, and Shimaoka uses only a few decorative brushstrokes to highlight a piece of this nature.

He has also made some fine pieces using simple patterns of contrasting glazes. These warm and harmonious glazes in gray tones are particularly beautiful, ranging from an olive gray through a pale blue gray.

Shimaoka uses the wheel, and his wares are mostly symmetrical and sturdily formed. He also uses molds, like Hamada, to hand-press his bottle forms, but he finishes them by the old Korean method of paddling them

121. *Dish by Shimaoka Tatsuzo in a checkerboard pattern in muted browns. D. 9".*
Signed storage box. Captain and Mrs. Roger Gerry

122. *An irregular shaped bowl by Shimaoka Tatsuzō. H. 2½". The rough surface*
is decorated with earth colors, a quiet rich green and brown, which blend harmoni-
ously. Captain and Mrs. Roger Gerry

into an oval form. The wooden paddles used for this process are carved with a variety of patterns, some of them very complex.

Funaki Michitada operates his family kiln near Matsu in the Fujina area of Shimane Prefecture. The Fujina district on the western end of Honshu is well known for its tradition of lead glazes; apart from kilns making Raku ware, there is only one other area in Japan that has this tradition. Funaki and other potters of the district have been deeply influenced by the work of Hamada and Leach in the English slipware and Korean traditions, and they have adapted their lead glazes to produce wares with a bright yellow or creamy white glaze. Funaki has made many beautiful pieces in the shape and colors of English slipware.

His son, Funaki Kenji (born 1927), also works at the family kiln, but his wares show a more modern trend. One of his methods of decoration is with a wooden stamping wheel, and he has made some very effective designs with it. He also decorates his wares with simple drawings of fish, birds, horses, and so on.

The Kyoto potter Kawai Kanjiro was born in 1890 in Yasugi, Shimane Prefecture. Like Hamada, he was trained as an engineer at the Tokyo Institute of Technology, and

123. Two covered pots. Left: *8" pot by Hamada Shōji.* Right: *pot with* temmoku *glaze and wax resist decoration by Kawai Kanjiro. D. 4¾".* Fogg Art Museum

124. Square tray on four feet. Kawai Kanjiro. Courtesy, Museum of Fine Arts, Boston, Morse Memorial Fund

125. Bowl by Kawai Kanjiro is white pottery covered with cream and brown glaze; motifs in brown. Courtesy of the Brooklyn Museum, Anonymous Gift

he was twenty-seven when he decided in 1917 to become an artist-potter in Kyoto.

A bold experimenter, he made technically excellent wares in a wide variety of styles. His pieces range from traditional Chinese-style *temmoku* (Ill. 123) and celadon, through wares inspired by the *mingei* movement in the 1930s, to semicubist shapes decorated with modern abstract designs in relief and splashed with harsh-colored glazes. He is particularly noted for his colors, and those of his middle period in the late 1930s are in soft lovely shades. The wares of his folk art period were inspired by Korean wares of the Yi Dynasty. He made pieces with beautiful simple shapes at this time and they are decorated in tasteful abstract designs with a light touch, usually against a soft gray, brown, or blue background (Ill. 124). He also made many tea ceremony pieces (Ill. 125).

He was a master of the style of superimposed glaze painting, in which the glaze colors of the decoration sink into the overall glaze coating and form one smooth coat of glaze. He also made frequent use of wax resist as a means of decoration (Ill. 123). Like Hamada, he used molds to hand-press earthenware and stoneware slabs into bottle forms.

After his folk art period, Kawai experimented with monochrome wares decorated with abstract designs in flat relief. His glazes at this time were marked by a deepening of the colors; the designs stand out in whitish contrast to the overall color. Later, he exaggerated this technique so that his designs covered the whole surface in a kind of relief sculpture.

At the end of his life (he died on November 18, 1966), Kawai was making pieces in semicubist shapes (Ill. 126) and using harsh-colored glazes in shades of orange, green, and brown. Besides the large quantity of wares he produced, Kawai wrote a number of books as well as many articles on the art of pottery. He also taught students.

In studying Kawai's work one can sense the restless spirit always in quest of further development, never satisfied, feeling that there is always more to discover. It seems to me that if we criticize some of his pieces he probably would have agreed with us—it must have been his critical appraisal of his own work that led him onward through a lifetime of experiment.

Kawai Hirotsugu (born in 1919), Kawai Kanjiro's son-in-law, is the successor to the family tradition. He is a member of the Crafts Department of the Kokugakai Association. Kawai Takeichi, nephew of Kawai Kanjiro, also works in folkcraft style (Ill. 127). Kawai Seitoku (born in 1927) is a mem-

126. Ewer, Kawai Kanjiro. The design, in tones of beige and brown, gives the illusion of a cockscomb. Captain and Mrs. Roger Gerry

ber of both the Nitten Exhibition and the Japan Decorative Arts Association.

Arao Tsunezo, one of Kawai Kanjiro's students, is a Kyoto potter and member of the Mingei Association. He has made Jō-mon-style wares decorated with cord patterns, but unlike Shimaoka and Kato Mineo he does not glaze or inlay the pattern with slip, and in consequence his wares are more in the original style. Both Arao Tsunezo and Ueda Tsuneji, another of Kawai Kanjiro's students, have done interesting work in *neriage*, or clay mosaic. This method of pressing clays of different colors into a mold results in the same pattern appearing on both inside and outside of the piece. Kimura Ichiro of Mashiko has used the *neriage* process to make bottle forms.

127. Left: *Square covered box with black and brown* temmoku; *Kawai Hirotsugu. H. 5½".* Right: *Square molded dish by Kawai Takeichi.* Fogg Art Museum

11

Contemporary Styles

The Nitten school made its appearance in 1927, when a group of ceramics was shown in the handicraft section of the Teiten Exhibition, and several master craftsmen were chosen as members of the government-organized Teikoko Bijutsuin. Potters in this group work in many styles; their work has had a great influence on new trends in Japanese ceramics. In 1935 the Ministry of Education sponsored the Buntei Exhibition to show these new-style ceramics, and subsequently organized a Nitten Exhibition. The Nitten Kogei-bu (the Craft Department of Nitten) was founded in 1958.

Since World War II, many different craft associations have been formed and most potters in Japan are members of one or other trend is toward abandoning the common more of these associations. Tomimoto formed the Shinshō-kai (New Craftsmen's Group) in 1947. The Sōdei-sha was founded in 1948, the Nippon Kogei-kai (Japan Art Crafts Association) in 1955, and the Gendai Kogei Bijutsu-ka-kyokai (Japan Decorative Arts Association) in 1961. There is also an association for women potters.

There are two trends of thought among potters working in the various associations. The trend of one group is to create wares intended for daily use, and these wares are in contemporary styles that have been evolved from the traditional styles. As the potters come from such diverse backgrounds, the styles are consequently very varied. The

128. Figure of a cormorant, by Kawashima Tennozan. Twentieth century. Black lustrous glaze, with white neck. L. 16¼". Metropolitan Museum of Art, Rogers Fund

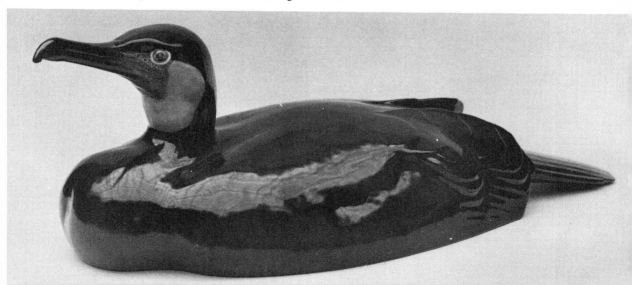

129. Teapot with cover. Stoneware, with brown iron glaze over pale yellow gray celadon. C. 1930–1935. Victoria and Albert Museum

cept of wares for practical use and experimenting with free and pure forms, but again generally in the framework of one of the traditional styles.

Kano Mitsue (born in Kyoto in 1903) won a Nitten Exhibition prize in 1949 for a white glazed jar with carved design. Asami Ryuzo (born in Kyoto in 1904) has a white porcelain jar on permanent exhibition in the Düsseldorf Museum. Kusube Yaichi of Kyoto (born 1897), a "national living treasure" and trustee of the Nitten Exhibition, carves and models his wares in low relief. The designs are generally of leaves or flowers, but he also makes use of abstract motifs. Imai Masayuki of Kyoto (born 1930) has decorated wares with designs reminiscent of those used by American Indians. (At this juncture I would like to say that I have seen "Indian pottery" for sale in the Badlands of South Dakota marked "made in Japan." Perhaps during their brief sojourn in Japan these ersatz Indian wares left a slight influence on Japanese pottery!)

Interesting methods of glaze and biscuit decoration are used by many potters who are searching for new means of expression but have not broken radically with the old ways. Uchida Kunio has developed a new *neriage* process, which he uses with artistic effect. His method is to press slices of contrasting colored clay into the surface of a partly shaped piece; the decoration thus

130. Stoneware water jar. Twentieth century. H. 20¾". Philadelphia Museum of Art, given by Mr. and Mrs. John F. Lewis; Photograph by A. J. Wyatt

131. Stoneware jar by Ishakawa Kinya, a Japanese potter working in Bucherville, Quebec. Modern. Collection of Cindy Stone

formed appears on only one surface of the ware, instead of going right through the biscuit. Ito Suiko has made some remarkably beautiful porcelains with glaze inlay, a very difficult process, and his graceful designs are carried out in delicate colors. Another potter who has developed a high degree of skill in glaze decoration is Tokuriki Magosaburo, who has produced striking effects with his superimposed glaze painting.

Other forms of decoration are produced in the body of the ware. Fujihira Shin coil-builds angular pots decorated with a form of appliqué. The motif, cut from a thin slice of clay, is attached to the pot; it makes a decoration in low relief, generally of human figures, birds, or animals, which are angular like the pots. Tsuji Shindoku makes use of an extended coil of wire to make interesting surface patterns on the body of his wares; he also creates patterns with a comb. Both Shinkai Kanzan and Taniguchi Ryozo use stamps to make impressed decorations on their wares.

Asao Gen, Sozen II, makes unglazed wares with a glossy surface produced by

burnishing. His wares have *unka* decoration ("cloud flower"), which is caused by carbon impregnation during the firing. In 1944 he was appointed by the Japanese government as technical expert and preserver of the art of *unka* ware.

Since World War II young potters have been experimenting with totally new concepts and expression in ceramics. Abstract designs, free-form shapes, as well as forms apparently inspired by the machine age and the robot, all vie for our attention. Only time will tell which of these will pass the test of acceptance by future generations and which will quietly sink into oblivion. However, I would like to point out that inventiveness in creating new forms does not necessarily produce a work of art; a piece must possess certain aesthetic qualities, not merely the ability to shock.

Notable among the avant-garde are four Kyoto potters, all members of the Sōdei-sha group, and all working with free-form or abstract shapes. They are Kumakura Junkichi (born 1920), Yamada Hikaru (born 1924), Hayashi Yasuo (born

132. A ceramic exhibition held in a gallery at a department store in Japan. Embassy of Japan, London

1928), and Hayashi Hideyuki (born 1937). Kumakura is well known for his ceramic sculpture. Susuki Osamu, also of Kyoto (born 1926), Satonaka Hideto of Tokyo (born 1932), and Miwa Ryusaku of Hagi, Yamaguchi Prefecture (born 1940), also belong to the Sōdei-sha group, but work in a less radical style.

Araki Takako of Nishinomiya, Hyogo Prefecture (born 1921), and Tsuboi Asuka of Kyoto (born 1932) are members of the Women's Association of Ceramic Art. Their work has received very favorable comment in the press. In 1971 both submitted works that were accepted competitively for exhibition in the Japan Ceramic Art Exhibition organized by the Mainichi newspapers. In the exhibition of contemporary ceramic art of Japan held in 1972 in several cities in the United States and Canada, Araki Takako was represented by four silk-screen printed bowls, and Tsuboi Asuka by "Sleeve Series A" and "Sleeve Series B" decorated in overglaze enamels.

Kato Seiji of Shigaraki, Shiga Prefec-

ture (born 1926), Mishima Kimiko of Osaka (born 1932), Yanagihara Mutsuo of Kyoto (born 1934), Koie Ryoji of Tokoname (born 1938), and Kuze Kenji of Seto (born 1945) are all independent potters working in freeform style.

Exhibitions by contemporary potters are held frequently in Japan and they are always well attended by an interested public. The Kyoto Art Museum held a large exhibition of this nature in 1968 that received considerable attention in the press.

Many department stores have large exhibition halls, and ceramic exhibitions are frequently held in these (Ill. 132). Generally the wares exhibited are by artists belonging to one group or another, but in 1971 the Mainichi newspapers celebrated their centenary by organizing the Japan Ceramic Art Exhibition, which showed wares made by contemporary potters working in all styles. This exhibition was shown in eight cities in Japan, and in 1972 seventy pieces were selected from the exhibition and were shown in the United States and Canada.

For Export Only

12

Japan in the Meiji Era (1868-1912)

Commodore Matthew C. Perry steamed along the coast of Japan on the morning of July 8, 1853. He had two steamers and two sloops under his command, and the people of Shimoda, seeing the black smoke, thought that the foreign ships on the horizon were on fire. They ran up the mountain behind the town for a better look, and as the early morning haze lifted, saw that the smoke was pouring from smokestacks rising up above the decks and that, marvelously, the ships were moving against the wind. Steamships were a new invention, and these were the first that the Japanese had ever seen. However, even more frightening to the Japanese than the strangeness of the ships were the many guns they carried, and these were pointing at the shore. Messengers were sent along the beach to Edo—mountains lay behind Shimoda, and the way to Edo was along the beach.

Although the Dutch at Nagasaki had told the Japanese that an American expedition to their country had been discussed in American and European newspapers, no one in Japan had believed the barbarians would really come. Confusion reigned in Edo. Some officials said the barbarians must be driven away, but others, who had seen the guns, knew that this would not be possible.

Orders were given for shore batteries to be manned, and black and white cloth screens were strung along the shore in front of the forts to hide the defenses. As there had been no wars for two hundred years, weapons were not in readiness for this sudden emergency. The townspeople ran in all directions, taking their valuables for safekeeping to friends who lived farther off.

On his flagship, the *Susquehanna*, Commodore Perry carried a letter from President Millard Fillmore to high officials in Japan. The letter asked the Japanese to break their long seclusion and enter into friendly relations with the United States. It also asked that shipwrecked American seamen be treated with kindness, and ports opened to supply coal and provisions to the whalers on the North Pacific and to steamers going between California and China. Trade was suggested, as well.

Commodore Perry relished the idea of the Japanese visit, for he felt it was highly appropriate that Americans should effect the opening of Japan to the world. Columbus had been on his way to Japan, inspired by the maps of Marco Polo, when he discovered America—it was fitting for the American people to finish what he had begun. Commodore Perry also had a sense of the dramatic.

On the way to Japan Perry paid a visit to Okinawa as a rehearsal; he landed there with bands playing, and even had himself carried to the palace in a sedan chair constructed by the ship's carpenter. But his visit had not been welcomed. The islanders sent messengers saying that the Queen Dowager was sick. The commodore did not believe this, however, and informed them that the music and pageantry would do her good. After considerable negotiation the regent

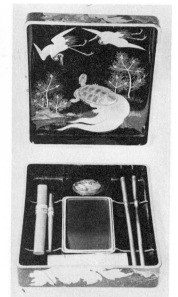

133. Two gifts from the emperor of Japan to Commodore Matthew C. Perry: a lacquer clothing box and a lacquer writing box (opened to show the inside). Peabody Museum of Salem; Photograph by M. W. Sexton

agreed to receive Perry at the palace, but the Queen Dowager did not appear. This was not really surprising, as—although the excuse had been that she was indisposed after receiving a British naval officer who had behaved in a rude and rambunctious manner —it was said that, in actual fact, she had died five years before.

As they steamed up the Japanese coast to Edo Bay, Commodore Perry looked through his glass at the shore batteries—the cloth screens did not hide much from his telescope. The clans had hoisted flags emblazoned with the crests of the noble houses, but what cannons there were were short-ranged and antiquated. The noise was nonetheless nerve-racking. When the foreign ships had neared the coast the Japanese on the shore had begun to beat their war gongs; the Americans had never heard the like.

After the ships anchored in Edo Bay, negotiations began for the delivery of the letter. Perry refused to see any minor official, saying that he could meet only with someone of equal rank to himself—he had given himself the title of Lord of the Forbidden Interior. It took several days to convince the Japanese that Perry would not be trifled with. Finally it was agreed that the commodore would deliver the letter to Prince Toda, as representative of the emperor.

On the designated day the Lord of the Forbidden Interior stepped from his ship onto his barge and was rowed ashore. Accompanied by martial music played by the brass band on the flagship, an imposing procession marched between the honor guard composed of the ships' crews. The marines led the way, then the sailors, followed by the commodore, who walked between two tall Negroes (most Japanese had never seen a Negro). The commodore also had a bodyguard of the ten biggest men in the fleet. They marched to the reception hall, and the letter, which had been carried from the ship in an ornate rosewood box by two midshipmen, was delivered in solemn silence. In return, the commodore was presented with a scroll in Japanese saying that, since President Fillmore's letter had now been delivered, the Americans should take their departure.

After the commodore had returned to his ship, the vessels did not depart immediately; instead, they remained nearby at anchor for another eight days, and conducted a survey of the coast. When that was completed, the commodore sailed away with his fleet. He planned to return the following spring for an answer.

The shogun (the title meant "barbarian-subduing generalissimo") did not know what to do, so he did something that no shogun

134. Bowl showing Yokohama in Kanagawa Prefecture, decorated by Kogetsu of Tokyo about 1860. Eight large foreign ships are in the harbor, towering over the small Japanese boats. Peabody Museum of Salem

had done in six hundred years. He sent to Kyoto to ask the advice of the emperor. Of course the emperor and his court had not seen the ships and the guns, and they sent back the message: "Expel the barbarians."

When Perry returned in February 1854 with his full complement of ten ships, the shogunate had no choice but to start negotiations. This they did with much feasting on their part (the commodore did not care too much for their food) and with entertainment provided by both sides. Whenever Perry felt that the negotiations were not proceeding to his liking, he threatened to sail up to Edo with his ships and his guns, whereupon the difficulties would vanish.

Shimoda and Hakodate were to be opened as ports, and Perry sailed to Shimoda to inspect that small town. The harbor was good, and they were struck by the beauty of the place. They did not realize immediately, however, that Shimoda had been offered because the mountains behind the town almost shut it off from the rest of Japan.

In June Perry sailed away again, and Japan started on the tremendous leap forward that was to transform her within a hundred years from a backward isolated country into a great modern power. She was

no longer the country at the very end of the world: unreachable, unapproachable, and self-sufficient. The Suez Canal had just been opened, and European ships bound for Japan were now able to make the voyage in a much shorter time than when they had been obliged to go around the Cape of Good Hope. And, of course, Japan lay on the way of American ships going west.

Within two years of Perry's departure, England, Russia, and Holland negotiated similar treaties with Japan, and steady trade developed between those countries and Japan. Foreigners were allowed to live in and trade at five ports, as well as at Osaka and Edo, and the fishing village of Yokohama grew rapidly as foreign merchants began to set up business there (Ill. 134).

For the next decade Japan suffered internal struggles between those who wanted to expel the foreigners and those who knew it was impossible. In 1867, however, after some short sharp battles, the Tokugawa was defeated and the shogun resigned. In 1868 the name Edo was changed to Tokyo, meaning "eastern capital," and the fifteen-year-old emperor, his court, and government moved to the Tokugawa Palace there the next year.

135. *Koda wares, 1870, from the Morse Collection. Edward S. Morse said, in his* Catalogue of the Morse Collection of Japanese Pottery, *that these wares bear the impressed mark* Gen *(Minamoto) and represent the work of the best potter of Koda in the 1870s.* Courtesy, Museum of Fine Arts, Boston, Morse Collection, Gift by Contribution

The new era was given the name Meiji; the emperor was given the title posthumously, after he died in 1912.

The new leaders realized that Japan was far behind the West and would have to modernize as fast as possible. Groups of students were sent to various Western countries to study the methods used there, and foreign teachers and technicians were brought to Japan. This period of learning was comparable, but on a much larger scale, to the time when Chinese civilization was taken to Japan a thousand years earlier.

After modern Western methods had been adopted, Japanese industry held a unique position in the world. The combination of cheap oriental labor harnessed to Western science produced low-priced goods of excellent quality, although a great many articles of poor quality were also made. The revival abroad of interest in Japanese ways created an almost insatiable market for her exports.

With the opening of Japan, tours of the Far Eastern countries became very popular with both Americans and Europeans of comfortable means. Japan owes the survival of her great artistic heritage to these first foreign visitors, who recognized her art treasures as such. In the mad rush for Western ideas these masterpieces would have been entirely lost without the efforts of such people as Edward Morse, William Sturgis Bigelow, and Ernest Fenollosa.

In the United States there are two important collections of Japanese pottery assembled by Edward Morse. The larger one is at the Museum of Fine Arts, Boston (Ill. 135); the smaller at the Peabody Museum in Salem, Massachusetts. Morse visited kilns throughout Japan, and his collections represent all types of Japanese pottery.

Edward Sylvester Morse, born on June 18, 1838, in Portland, Maine, was a natural collector. He started as a boy with a collection of land shells, which was so comprehensive by the time he was fifteen that other collectors came to see it from as far as Boston and even England.

As a young man, Morse studied zoology under Louis Agassiz at Harvard. He was one of the young student assistants at Harvard's newly built Museum of Comparative Zoology, one of his duties being cataloging and arranging specimens. At Agassiz's suggestion he began a study of brachiopods, tracing their development from fossil to living species, and it was this study that eventually took him to Japan. However, before this —and soon after Harvard—he was appointed a member of the staff of the newly established museum in Salem, Massachusetts. George Peabody had given $140,000 "for the promotion of science and useful knowledge in the county of Essex," and this provided for the purchase of the East India Marine Hall in Salem, owned by the East

India Marine Society, and the establishment of a museum there. (Later, Morse was curator of the museum from 1868 to 1871, director from 1880 to 1914, and director emeritus from 1914 to 1925.)

Morse was a highly succesful lecturer who toured the country speaking on natural history. During one of his tours, late in the spring of 1874 in San Francisco, he heard of Japan's many varieties of brachiopods, but three years passed before he could arrange a three months' visit there to collect specimens.

Morse arrived at Yokohama in June 1877, and at once took a train on the newly constructed railroad to Tokyo to present a letter of introduction to Dr. David Murray, superintendent of the Mombusho (Department of Education). On the way he noticed some fossilized shells lying beside the tracks, and at once recognized that the construction of the railroad bed had unearthed a prehistoric kitchen midden. In Tokyo he told members of the university faculty about the shells and aroused their interest. Archaeology was unknown in Japan at that time, and it was this discovery by Morse that initiated the study.

Dr. Murray took Morse to meet Professor Toyama, a Cornell graduate, and Vice-Minister Tanaka, and both were impressed with Morse's knowledge and personality. When Dr. Murray and Morse returned from a brief trip to Nikko, Japanese authorities asked Morse to remain in Japan and organize a department of zoology at the university and to found a museum of natural history. He accepted a two-year contract at the Imperial University in Tokyo, and was also given the staff to found a marine biological laboratory at Enoshima, the first in the Pacific regions. The laboratory was a rented fisherman's hut!

Morse's interest in Japanese pottery began—this, too, happened by chance—a year later. He was having trouble with his nerves and digestion, and his doctor prescribed a daily five-mile walk. When Morse objected to such a regimen, the doctor suggested that he find a hobby to pursue on his walks, and a few days later Morse discovered Japanese pottery. The first pieces were saucers made in the form of certain shells, which Morse found in the various Japanese shops he passed on his walks. When he showed the saucers to Japanese friends, they told him the pieces were neither old nor from famous potteries, and their attitude made him aware that the Japanese appreciated only the best in pottery.

His friends took him to gatherings of connoisseurs, who amused themselves by guessing the origin of various pieces of pottery handed from one guest to the other. Each guest wrote down the origin, date, and potter's name, and at the end of the game there was a prize for the winner. Morse soon realized that this game was built on exact knowledge—the connoisseurs had to be able to recognize the clays used, the kiln, the techniques, and the style. Resolving to learn all these things, he became the pupil of Noritane Ninagawa, who had written an unpublished book on the subject. Every Sunday afternoon for the next year, until Ninagawa died, Morse took a pottery lesson.

During this period the Japanese were avidly learning from the West, and ignoring or forgetting their ancient arts and customs; the tea ceremony was forgotten for a quarter of a century. Collections in the hands of old families were being dispersed to help their owners out of financial straits. In time, when the Japanese came again to value their ancient heritage, they found that many of their treasures had vanished from their land, never to be recovered. That some remained —and the recognition of their artistic value —were in great part due to Morse, as we shall see later.

Morse came to know Japan very well, traveling to places that no other foreigner had seen. He served as a scientific adviser to the government, and in that capacity had the freedom to travel anywhere he wished. His journal, published later under the title of *Japan Day by Day*, related adventures of all kinds: nearly being caught in a bear trap that held a poisoned arrow, eating raw marine worms for supper, searching for ancient pottery while up to his waist in water in a dark cave under an avalanche of huge poisonous centipedes. His descriptions of these adventures delighted his lecture audiences during the three years he spent in America after his return in 1879.

Those years (1879–1882) were busy ones for Morse. Not only did he give his highly successful lectures; he was appointed director of the Peabody Museum in Salem. However, he missed Japan, and with the ostensible purpose of forming an ethnological collection for the Peabody Museum, as well as adding to his pottery collection, he returned there in 1882, traveling with Dr. William Sturgis Bigelow, whom he had persuaded to visit that country.

Dr. Bigelow was the son of the well-known physician Henry Jacob Bigelow, a founder of the Museum of Fine Arts in Boston. In Japan the younger Dr. Bigelow became interested in Japanese art and assembled a large collection of lacquer, swords, and sword guards, which later was given to the Museum of Fine Arts in Boston.

In Tokyo, joined by Ernest Fenollosa and Okakura Kakuzō, Morse and Bigelow undertook a journey to the great art centers of Japan. The railroad had not yet been extended very far, so they went by jinrikisha and boat through the southern provinces. Morse wrote:

We shall see a little of the life of old Japan. I shall add a great many specimens to my collection of pottery. Dr. Bigelow will secure many forms of swords, guards and lacquers, and Mr. Fenollosa will increase his remarkable collection of pictures, so that we will have in the vicinity of Boston by far the greatest collection of Japanese art in the world.

Okakura Kakuzō, the only Japanese in the party, acted as interpreter. He had learned English as a child. His father, a samurai who had been obliged to open a silk-thread store after the collapse of the feudal system, recognized the importance of learning English for his business, and wanted his sons to learn it also. Okakura Kakuzō proved to be an apt pupil. In due course he entered the Tokyo Institute of Foreign Languages, which became Tokyo University in 1877. Okakura attended the class in Western

philosophy taught by Fenollosa, and because of his fluency in English often acted as class interpreter.

When Fenollosa became interested in Japanese art, he had Okakura translate old books on art and artists for him, and later when he lectured on art at gatherings in Tokyo, Okakura interpreted for him. At these gatherings Fenollosa praised the simplicity of Japanese paintings, and pointed out that the effect created by this artistic simplicity was superior to the masses of color in Western oil paintings. He reproached the Japanese for ignoring their own art in their rush to learn about Western art, which they were accepting without question as being better than their own.

Through the efforts of Fenollosa, Okakura, and others of the same opinion, an Imperial Commission of Fine Arts was established to record, catalog, and study the existing art collections in Japan, many of which were in temples. Fenollosa and Okakura were both named commissioners of fine arts, and traveled together to various parts of Japan in their official capacity. (One of their greatest discoveries was the standing Buddha at Nara, ascribed to the days of Suiko [A.D. 593–629], which had not been seen for centuries.)

In 1882, when they had joined Morse and Bigelow for the trip to the great art centers, a chance remark made by Morse had a far-reaching influence on Okakura. Morse remarked that it was sad so much fine Japanese art was now on the market—it was as if the lifeblood of Japan were seeping from a hidden wound. The words had a profound effect. When Okakura returned to Tokyo he tried to make the authorities and people with influence do something about the unfortunate situation. Two years later, in 1884, through his efforts the law of Koku-Ho (national treasures) was enacted. All the remaining treasures of ancient art were registered and were restricted from export, most of them becoming in due course part of the collections in the Tokyo, Nara, and Kyoto museums.

During his time as professor at Tokyo University, Morse's forthright manner earned him the trust of the university presi-

dent, Baron Kato. Many bombastic foreigners came to the university, ready to accept
well-paid posts that they were not academi-
cally qualified to hold. In his usual out-
spoken way Morse told the president of the
situation, and was asked to name suitable
candidates for the vacant posts. This he did,
either nominating competent people he
knew personally or getting recommenda-
tions from those whose judgment he trusted.

Many of the people recommended by
Morse, once in Japan, became interested in
oriental art in one form or another, and
made collections of their own. Most of these
collections were eventually deposited in the
Museum of Fine Arts, Boston, making that
museum host to the largest single collection
of oriental art in the world. This collection,
in turn, has had its influence on other collections, and so Morse can be thanked for con-
tributing in some way to the collections of
oriental art in this country and around the
world. This is particularly interesting in
view of the fact that Morse is so often reproached for a lack of aesthetic taste and
judgment.

The two Japanese pottery collections
made by Edward Morse are the largest collections of their kind in the world outside
Japan. An Englishman, J. L. Bowes, made a
similar collection, but it was not as extensive
and has since been dispersed.

Morse spent twenty years making his

first pottery collection. He traveled all over
Japan, visited pottery kilns throughout the
country, and collected examples of their
products. In 1890 he sold this collection to
the Museum of Fine Arts in Boston for the
sum of $76,000; the collection is still there in
the cases the way he arranged it.

When he became director of the Peabody Museum in Salem, Morse set about
making a duplicate collection (Ill. 136). This
too is a large collection, but it is not as complete as the one in Boston.

The Museum of Fine Arts in Boston
and the Peabody Museum in Salem were intended as sister museums as far as their oriental collections were concerned, with the
Peabody Museum as host for the ethnic (arts
and crafts) collections. However, nowadays,
certain items are considered to belong more
rightfully in the Fine Arts section, although
at the time of acquisition they were considered ethnic. Anyone interested in Japanese
pottery should try to visit one of these collections, which are not widely enough
known. The Edward Sylvester Morse Collection in Boston's Museum of Fine Arts is,
however, housed in a part of the museum's
third floor that is not open to the public.
Visitors are requested to make an appoint-
ment with the Department of Asiatic Art to
see the collection; a letter or phone call is
necessary before a visit.

At the Peabody Museum in Salem, a

136. *Three pieces from the Morse Collection.* Left: *dish, Tanzan, 1870; raised floral decoration is pink, blue,
yellow, and green.* Center: *jar with heavy drip glaze; Iga, 1870.* Right: *bottle with blue and brown decoration
on beige background; Iga, 1880.* Peabody Museum of Salem; Photo by M. W. Sexton

PLATE 1. *Pre-Nippon wares: Dish with lace decoration in raised slip has white enamel edging and beading and herbaceous peonies,* shakuyaku. *The glaze is heavy. Inscribed* Shigeki Imanari *in Japanese characters. The covered vegetable dish with Chinese-style design at first glance looks Chinese, but besides the Japanese inscription underneath that reads* Shunkō, *the colors are brighter and the men are wearing Japanese clothing,* kariginu, *and hats,* eboshi.

PLATE 2. *Nippon bowl, Chinese-style design, with vivid Japanese colors.*

PLATE 3. *Satsuma vase, h. 25". Rim is ornamented with knife cuts.*

PLATE 4. *Detail of decoration on the Satsuma vase showing color rubbed into the crackle on one petal of the peony and on the bamboo trunk above it.*

PLATE 5. *Satsuma temple jar. H. 33".*

PLATE 6. *Pre-Nippon vase. In-tricate coralene beading is deco-rated with gold. There is ex-cellent brushwork on both the floral decoration and the shaded background. Underglaze blue is imported cobalt oxide.*

PLATE 7. *Chocolate pot, pre-Nippon ware. Although there is considerable fluting on the body, the handle is very plain.*

PLATE 8. *Small Imari pitcher, late nineteenth cen-tury, Chinese pheasant design. The underglaze blue is the native cobalt, gosu.*

PLATE 9. *Nippon M-in-Wreath vase with beautifully painted sunset landscape scene. A characteristic of these fine wares is that although the principal motif (in this case a landscape) is painted with infinite care and attention to detail, the border decoration is often somewhat irregular.*

PLATE 10. Left, *footed cup and saucer with Satsuma-style decoration of Chinese scenes; saucer inscribed* Haruta *in Japanese characters.* Center, *condensed milk jar, with hole underneath, and oriental-looking handles. Inscribed* Shimamura *in Japanese characters.* Right, *cup and saucer with delicately painted design of lady and child.*

PLATE 11. *Chocolate set with Nippon Maple Leaf mark. Chocolate sets had five cups until World War I, when sets with six cups began to be made. This set has handles of unusual shape.* Mrs. Anne Burley

PLATE 12. *Kutani chocolate set decorated with five scenes in reserves shaped like a folding fan, lantern, flat (Chinese) fan, ancient mirror, and cherry blossom. Each scene depicts a season: the landscape view with cherry blossoms is for spring; an old lady seated on the floor by the open* shōji *represents summer (her eyebrows are painted in the shape of a* V, *which was the conventional means used in old prints to show age in a woman); a scene with red maples represents autumn; the other two scenes with pine trees depict winter.*

PLATE 13. *Four pieces of pre-Nippon, all unmarked. Plate,* Mr. and Mrs. D. Stone. *Vase and cup,* Mr. and Mrs. T. M. Lotito

PLATE 14. *Two Nippon pieces with European-style decoration. Vase at left has completely symmetrical decoration. Both back and front are exactly the same, an unusual characteristic. The mark is Kinjo Nippon. The footed dish with bluebirds carries the Rising Sun mark; usually Rising Sun pieces have pastel floral decoration.*

PLATE 15. *Two Satsuma-style vases. In contrast to the Nippon pieces, which portray human figures as types (man, woman, child), the people on Satsuma wares look like individuals.*

PLATE 16. *Pair of Nippon M-in-Wreath vases, front and back views. The overglaze enamel decoration resembles cloisonné.*

PLATE 17. *Four Nippon M-in-Wreath pieces, c. World War I. All are imitative of European wares, but their oriental origin is apparent. The porcelain of the sugar and creamer is of excellent quality.*

PLATE 18. *Nippon Maple Leaf wares: The small bowl must have been shaped by hand after it was taken from the mold—one can feel how the potter pressed the rim between his thumb and fingers to make a fluted edge. Vase in European style—Veronica Kiley*

PLATE 19. *Nippon vases. The gray porcelain has been deepened and shaded to make a beautiful soft background for the floral decoration. Left (anemones), Imperial mark. Center (poppies), t"t" mark. Right (mixed blossoms), Imperial mark. Mr. and Mrs. J. Schrody*

PLATE 20. *This set carries the Nippon Hō-ō bird mark; it is made of good quality porcelain. Although the cups appear to be teacups, the pot is the size of a chocolate pot.* Mrs. Robert Seekamp

PLATE 21. *A bisque figurine of winged cherub playing the concertina is marked "Made in Occupied Japan."* Pinney Collection

PLATE 22. *The cups in this set are good quality porcelain. The extensive multicolored molded decoration is obviously designed to appeal to the Western market. Note the elaborate gold handles and the overabundance of gold decoration inside the cups. Mark: Occupied Japan.* Mr. and Mrs. T. M. Lotito

137. Blue and white bowl, Meiji Period (c. 1880). Collection of Jiromaru-no-Toyohashi. *Garden seat, Kyushu; also Meiji Period. The hexagonal sides are alternating blue and white and celadon.* Captain and Mrs. Roger Gerry

much smaller museum, the limited space makes it impossible to show more than a selection of the specimens from the Morse collection in the public galleries, but the exhibits are changed at frequent intervals. This collection is an extraordinarily interesting one, well worth traveling some distance to see.

During his years in Japan, Morse had a great influence on Japanese education. In the scientific field, his lectures at Tokyo University were so successful that much of Japan's progress in medicine, in biological, botanical, and agricultural research, and in physics and archaeology is said to have stemmed from a group of ninety of his students.

Between his visits to Japan, Morse spend much of his time at home in the United States on lecture tours. His enthusiastic lectures, illustrated by ambidextrous drawings on a blackboard, fired his listeners to go to Japan and see the country for themselves. One such person was Mrs. Jack Gardner.

Isabella Stewart Gardner was the wife of Jack Gardner, whose family had owned sailing ships in Salem, and had moved to Boston when the merchant ships transferred to that port instead of Salem. His mother was a Peabody of Salem.

When Mrs. Gardner and her husband undertook an oriental tour in 1882, they had already heard a great deal about Japan while still in Boston. Besides the Morse lectures, they had a closer source of information: Mrs. Gardner's personal physician, Dr. Henry J. Bigelow, the father of William Sturgis Bigelow.

Isabella Gardner—or Mrs. Jack, as she was called—was a vivacious lady not in the least afraid to shock the staid matrons of Boston society. When William Sturgis Bige-

low met the Gardners in Japan in 1883, he described Mrs. Gardner as "gloom-dispeller, corpse reviver and general chirker-up." Her great interest, especially after her husband died, was her art collection, and in her later years she had a Venetian palace built on the Fenway in Boston, near the Museum of Fine Arts, to house the collection and later to become a museum. Her friends and protégés included artists of all kinds. Okakura gave her advice on oriental additions to her collection, and sent her a tea set (Ill. 23).

Okakura spent most of the last ten years of his life in Boston. In 1903 he became adviser to the Chinese and Japanese Department of the Museum of Fine Arts, and was appointed curator there in 1910, a post he held until his death in 1913.

Japanese and oriental influences in art were everywhere. Whistler, one of Mrs. Gardner's friends, who made a pastel portrait of her, which he called *A Little Note in Yellow*, had painted a picture of a Japanese room. John Singer Sargent, another of her friends, who painted more than one portrait of her, used two huge oriental vases as background in one of his famous portraits.

Japanese art had come into vogue in the

United States with the Centennial Exposition in Philadelphia in 1876. For this exposition the Japanese government sent a large collection of ceramics, the major part being devoted to showing the history and development of the art. However, I am told on good authority that many of the fine old pieces exhibited were not old pieces at all, but very skillfully made copies of the originals. A great many new-style pieces had been specially made for the exhibition, using the new processes the Japanese were fast learning from the West. The ceramic wares in the exhibition were subsequently shipped to London, where they can now be seen in the Victoria and Albert Museum.

By 1883 there was an exhibition of foreign wares in Boston for which a number of Japanese factories had sent examples of their ceramic work. The exhibition catalog mentioned—among others—Kiriu Kosho Kuarsha of Tokyo and Koransha of Arita.

138. Painting weights, twentieth century, to be hung on the lower corners of a painting (scroll) so that it does not curl up when on display. Philadelphia Museum of Art, given by Mrs. Edgar Stone; Photograph by A. J. Wyatt

13

Ceramic Methods since 1868

There is a vast difference between wares made in traditional Japanese style and those made since 1868 in Western style for export. Imari wares, described more fully in the earlier part of this book, continued to be decorated in the traditional style, but on account of the mass-production techniques introduced after 1868 the method of applying the decoration underwent various changes. In the 1880s some very poor pieces were made because the hand-painted decoration had to be done at high speed to fill the agent's orders. Later, the type of design used lent itself to machine-made perfection, resulting in perfect but artistically cold pieces. Satsuma-style wares, on the other hand, had an abundance of decoration, which even when meticulously executed is so heavy that it is often unattractive. This type of decoration, intended to please the taste of the foreigner, was completely misunderstood by the Japanese, and in many instances the resulting pieces pleased nobody's taste. An artist can make something of true beauty only when he works to satisfy his own standards.

After 1868 the Japanese also created a new style based on European methods, and turned out some very attractive pieces. This style lies somewhere between the Oriental and the Western. The colors and designs are European, but the workmanship is Japanese. Unfortunately, the period when the best of this work was done was very short, and by the time of the First World War it was over. That does not mean that afterward nothing

good was made for the export market. On the contrary, very good pieces were made, but the period of good work at nominal prices was over.

The finer wares of this period (1868–1918) have never been generally recognized as such. There are two reasons for this situation: the wares are not in the Japanese tradition; and, at the time they were being made, they sold for very little abroad. Of course, the low value was not based on poor quality, but rather that the people who made the wares were not paid in accordance with the time they spent or the quality of their work. Before 1868 Japanese craftsmen were supported by their local daimyos and could spend as long as necessary to make a beautiful article; time was of no importance. This tradition of meticulous work lingered for a while, but when craftsmen were paid only for what they produced, they could no longer afford to spend unlimited time on one object. The pressure, also, was intense from the agents who handled the selling abroad— articles had to be made as fast as possible.

The change from good careful handwork to the frenzy of mass production was accomplished in remarkably few years. Dr. Gottfried Wagner, a German chemist, went to Arita on 1870 to advise on European-style methods of ceramic production. Modern factory equipment was installed, and coal-burning kilns put in instead of wood-burning ones. Plaster molds were introduced, clay molds having been in use up to this

139. Powder box, unmarked, is good quality porcelain with pink roses, green border, and gold star decoration in the center. Pinney Collection. Nippon M-in-Wreath sugar and creamer with interesting oriental-looking shape are decorated in dull gold.

time. European enamel colors were also introduced, with their infinite possibilities of color shading, and European methods of glazing were demonstrated.

Foreign-style wares were in great demand by the Japanese; the traditional was pushed aside as worthless. After the emperor and his court moved to Edo in 1868, and the city was renamed Tokyo, the area became a center of foreign trade. Foreign diplomats and traders bought houses and demanded Western-style comforts and living conditions. The Japanese people, especially those around Tokyo and other centers of foreign trade, fell under this influence, and a craze for Western-style wares swept the country.

Prior to this time the Japanese had abhorred symmetry; tablewares had to be different, each piece contrasting with and enhancing the others. Now matched sets were bought and pairs of vases made—these had not existed for the Japanese people before the coming of foreign trade.

Kilns were set up in and around Tokyo expressly for the purpose of making Western-style wares. The new kilns were of two kinds: either kilns of individual potters producing their own particular style, potting, firing, and decorating each piece themselves; or decorator kilns, which were muffle kilns capable of sufficient heat only to fix the decoration. Wares made elsewhere were

140. Celery dish set; Nippon, M-in-Wreath. The large dish was made in a solid casting mold; the salt dishes in flopover molds. The decoration seems at first glance to be perfectly regular, but on closer inspection the Japanese love for irregularity becomes apparent—the roses are surrounded by leaves, some blue and some green, and no two sets are exactly alike. Gold is freely used.

brought "in the white" to Tokyo to be decorated for the foreign trade. Huge quantities of this type of ware were produced, as mass-production methods improved. Some pieces were marked with the name of the kiln, but the kilns were too numerous and small to be traced or classified, and many lasted for only a short period. Other marks, particularly for the American market, were import-export marks, and were either the symbol of the export company that gathered the pieces together for shipment or that of the importer.

To start with, the wares were fairly individual, but when plaster molds came into common use identical wares could be produced in large quantity.

Molds

Four main types of molds were used. Drain molds, which utilized a liquid slip (clay mixed with enough liquid so that it could be poured), were the most common, and were used for vases, teapots, chocolate pots, cups, and the like. Solid casting molds were also used with liquid slip, and these were for dishes, bowls, and so on (Ill. 140). Flopover molds called for a pancake of clay over the mold; they were used for shallow articles. Press molds, used for cup handles, required lumps of soft clay.

With whatever method used, the dry plaster of the mold absorbed sufficient liquid from the clay so that the molded piece became firm enough to be removed from the mold. The piece was then leather-hard, in the right state for other parts like spouts or handles to be attached to it with slip. All the

parts attached together had to be in the same state of hardness so that they would dry out at the same rate.

Drain Molds: This type of mold was made in the shape of the outside of the piece to be molded; liquid slip was poured into it and, after a few minutes, when a wall of the required thickness was formed on the inside of the mold, the excess slip was poured off. One piece—for instance, a teapot—might require a number of separate molds, depending on what had to be attached: a spout, handle, feet, stem, or finial. The disadvantage of this method is that it is not easy to make two pieces with walls of equal thickness, and the inside of the finished pieces is never as smooth as with other methods. For this reason cups intended for use are not made in this way anymore, but they were made in Japan by this method until the jigger came into general use in the early days of this century. A characteristic of pieces made in a drain mold is that, when a foot or stem is part of the mold and not attached separately afterward, the slip is pulled down into it and forms a hollow on the inside. Better pieces always have the stem molded separately and attached with slip when both parts are leather-hard. Good Meiji pieces were finished with great care, and it is usually hard to find the exact spot where two parts were joined together. The process of smoothing out the leather-hard pieces, or greenware, by hand is called fettling.

Drain molds were made in one piece or several, depending on the shape of the ware. A one-piece mold had to be shaped so that the molded piece would slip out once it was

141. *Chocolate set; Nippon, E-Oh mark. The chocolate pot, cups, and sugar bowl were made in drain molds, with the handles made in press molds and joined with slip. The saucers were made in solid casting molds. These pieces were made toward the end of the Nippon period (probably at the end of World War I), and the brushwork of the decoration was not done with the care used on the older pieces.*

dry. As this placed considerable restriction on the design of a piece, most drain molds were made in two or more pieces, divided at the thickest points, either horizontally or laterally. A two-piece mold can be used only to shape something that has a flat, or almost flat, bottom; a three-piece mold must be used if there is to be an indentation at the foot.

Chocolate pots were made with the lateral division. In the older pieces it is very hard to find any trace of a ridge, or "fettle," where the mold divided. The joint was generally concealed in an indentation in the design, if there was one handy. One has to search very carefully to find the joint in the better pieces; the best way to do so is to tilt the object in all directions in bright sunlight until some clue finally becomes visible. This usually takes the form of a slight line or depression in the biscuit or an irregularity in the glaze, although on poorly made pieces there may be evidence of a ridge. Tilting in bright sunlight is useful for finding many things. One can often read a mark that has been rubbed off in the course of time, as the light picks up the dullness of the glaze where the original mark was located.

I have dealt at length with the construction of drain molds and explained fettling, as an understanding of methods and techniques is necessary for anyone who wants to try to date the later export wares. After the turn of the century, corners were cut in order to turn goods out faster, and wares produced in the 1920s were often made very roughly. Finials were included in the drain mold of a lid, as were handles in the mold of the body, and the result was clumsy.

Solid casting: When a piece is made in a solid cast mold, it is shaped on both sides by the mold. This method has many advantages over drain casting, in that the inside does not have to conform to the outside. Cups and bowls do not have to be of the same thickness throughout; they can have a thicker base with tapering sides. The inside can be perfectly smooth, with no ring inside the foot, as in drain casting. In drain casting two pieces made in the same mold may be of a different thickness, but pieces that are solid cast are identical in form. Plates, cups, and bowls were solid cast.

The molds for solid casting are made in two parts, top and bottom. The slip used must be thicker than that used in drain molds, as excessive shrinkage is not desirable. The slip used for drain molds is about half clay and half water, and it undergoes great shrinkage as it dries out, an advantage in getting the piece out of the mold.

Flopover molds, or drape molds, are the simplest form of mold. They are used to make flat shapes. Only a one-piece mold is necessary, shaped like the inside of the piece,

142. *Bouillon set; Noritake, red M-in-Wreath mark. These wares were made with a jigger. The design is of the Noritake stylized type.*

but in reverse, convex instead of concave. A pancake of clay is rolled out and pressed over the mold. This produces flat-bottomed pieces, and the bottom is left unglazed, having no foot to stand on in the kiln. This type of mold was used for trays (Ills. 164, 209, and 217) and for small pieces like salt dishes (Ills. 220, 230, and many others).

Press Molds: These are mainly used for making handles, although sometimes for figurines. A press mold is made in two pieces, a front and a back. For a cup handle, a cylinder of soft clay is pressed between the two halves, and the excess squeezed out into a trough around the edge. When dry, the handle had to be fettled to remove the ridge where the two halves of the mold joined.

Jiggering: The commercial way of making plates and bowls is with the jigger, which consists of a plaster bat placed on a wheel and a template held by an arm. To make a plate or saucer, a convex bat is used to form the inside of the piece, the template being in the shape of the outside. A flat pancake of clay is placed on the bat, pressed down firmly, and the upper surface wet with a sponge. After the wheel is started, the jigger arm holding the template is lowered —it takes only a few seconds to form the outside of the plate (Fig. 3).

A bowl is made in the opposite way. The plaster bat is concave and forms the

Fig. 3. The jigger. Left: *A bat shaped like the inside of a plate is placed on the wheel. A pancake of clay is put on the bat; then the jigger arm with template attached to it is lowered. As the wheel spins, the outside of the plate is formed in a matter of seconds. The bat is then lifted off the wheel and the plate left to dry.* Right: *A bowl, or any deep piece, has to be done in the opposite way. The bat is shaped like the outside of the bowl; then a lump of clay is put in it and roughly pressed against the sides. The template is in the shape of the inside of the bowl, and as the wheel turns it forms the inside. The bowl is left in the bat to dry, and as it shrinks it pulls away from the side of the bat. Were it made in the same way as the plate, it would crack as it shrank in drying.*

outside of the bowl. (If it were done the other way, the bowl would crack open when it shrank in the drying process). A ball of clay is pressed onto the bottom of the plaster bat, and the potter works the clay up the sides with his fingers to make a rough bowl shape. Then he dampens the surface with a sponge and lowers the jigger arm holding the template. The template is, of course, in the shape of the inside of the bowl. Finally the bat is lifted off the wheel and the bowl left in it to dry.

These varying processes of molding the biscuit naturally make for variations in the type of body produced. The most beautiful effects resulted when a liquid slip was used, as the glazed surface had a smooth, slightly undulating appearance that caused it to gleam in the light. Pieces made from a pancake or ball of clay pressed against a mold have a duller, less smooth look, and are often somewhat grainy in appearance.

Decoration

Ceramics can be decorated in two different ways: either with clay, so that the decoration becomes part of the body, or with color. Clay decoration of the post-1868 export porcelains was mainly done through slip-trailing and coralene beading.

Slip-trailing results in a raised ridge of slip; the slip is trailed on when the ware is either leather-hard or in the biscuit state. When applied to leather-hard ware, it generally serves as a raised outline or decorative border for an enameled decoration, and is usually painted gold. Slip can also be applied after the glaze, and in this case the slip used is in one or more contrasting colors (Ill. 143). Slip-trailing was originally done with a bamboo tube, but a rubber syringe is often used now. More elaborate slip decoration was formed by hand and painstakingly applied to the surface of the ware. The Japanese call all these types of raised clay or enamel decoration *moriage*.

Coralene beading is done by a similar process. It consists of a series of dots instead of a continuous ridge, and is always enameled over, again generally in gold. The older pieces have extensive coralene beading, often in patterns using a variety of sizes of dots (Color Plate 6). Later inferior pieces have an

143. *Nippon vase, M-in-Wreath mark. The dragon decoration was made by slip-trailing; the dragon is in pale gray slip, and the Chinese-style flames are in turquoise slip. The piece has an interesting mottled gray and green background, the whole design being dominated by the brilliant turquoise blue enamel eyes of the dragon. Note the three claws on this Japanese dragon's visible foot (compare with Ill. 161, for a Chinese dragon).*

imitation coralene beading done with dots of enamel.

Colored decoration may be in the form of either colored glazes or underglaze or overglaze enamel designs. Sometimes several different colors are applied to the glaze to make an attractive variegated effect.

Underglaze Designs: Normally, the only color used for underglaze designs is blue; underglaze blue and white decoration is called *sometsuke* in Japanese. Cobalt blue is the only color that does not vary in shade according to the temperature of the firing. Other colors tend to run when used as underglaze colors.

Up to the latter part of the nineteenth century, the native *gosu* was used for blue. This is a pebble found in oriental riverbeds, which contains a mixture of cobalt, manganese, and iron. However, these days, imported cobalt oxide is generally used; it was first used at the Arita kilns in 1869.

Native Japanese *gosu* is very hard to find nowadays, and is much more difficult to apply than imported cobalt oxide. The ground *gosu* has to be mixed with a thick

144. Dish with raised handle; Nippon, M-in-Wreath. The blue cobalt oxide border has heavy gold decoration. Mr. and Mrs. T. M. Lotito

solution of green tea before it is used, as the tannin in the tea fixes the decoration so that it does not spread when the glaze is applied. Imported cobalt oxide is more reliable, cheaper, and stronger than native *gosu*, but has a much harsher and more brilliant color. *Gosu* is of a more gray blue color.

On post-1868 export wares cobalt oxide was used very often as a blue border, and the wares were then sent out "in the white" for decoration. The blue border was customarily decorated with a gold design (Ill. 144). This type of decoration was also used extensively on spouts and handles.

Overglaze Enamel Decoration: A similar type of border decoration, called *kinrande*, in red and gold, was used for Kutani and Kutani-style wares, and also on spouts and handles. The red background, however, was in overglaze enamels.

In the Meiji era, a cheap and efficient method was found for applying the red ground, and this was used for export wares. It consisted of painting the glaze surface with lacquer, and when this was partly dry, dusting on red enamel powder from a cloth bag. In this way an even coating was obtained without brush marks. The red enamel was then fired at a low temperature along with the rest of the overglaze enamel decoration, and after the firing the gold decoration was applied and the piece fired once again at a still lower temperature (Ill. 145). Gold has to be fired at a lower temperature than that used for enamel decoration; otherwise the gold will sink into the enamel and disappear.

As mass production increased and time and costs were cut, yellow enamel was used as a cheap substitute for gold. It could be painted on the red background as soon as that was dry, and they could both be fired together. A method of cutting costs without eliminating the use of gold was to apply the gold directly to the glaze, making sure that none of the gold touched or was on top of the enamel decoration. In this way the gold could be fired at the same time as the rest of the decoration, with no danger of its disappearing under the other colors (Ill. 146).

Gold was used lavishly on export wares of the Meiji Period. On older unmarked

145. Modern Kutani-style teapot. Gold chrysanthemum pattern on red ground decorates the spout. Mr. and Mrs. Elliott H. Fischer

146. *Berry bowl set, c. 1925. Although gold was used in this Kaga-style decoration, it was applied directly to the glaze, and nowhere over the enamels. The red rim is decorated with yellow enamel brushstrokes. This method eliminated an extra firing for the gold. The name of a small company appears on the underside in Japanese characters.*

148. *Detail from a Nippon M-in-Wreath vase, showing a finely painted landscape.*

147. *Vase, h. 9"; Nippon, Maple Leaf. This fine piece is beautifully painted, with much goldwork. The coralene beading is in two different sizes, which is a mark of good quality Nippon. This vase also illustrates the Japanese fondness for showing a scene as from some particular vantage point; here the landscape seems to be glimpsed through an ornate window.*

pieces it appears mainly over coralene beading or as a decoration on underglaze blue borders and handles. Kutani pieces have gold decoration on a red ground as well as considerable fine gold brushwork in the pictorial designs. Nippon wares have gold on coralene beading, which is generally not as ornate as on the older pieces; the beading is usually in one size or style, in contrast to the varied kinds used on the older wares. Nippon Maple Leaf pieces make heavy use of gold (Ill. 147), but Torii pieces have very little.

The styles and skills used in enamel decoration vary a great deal. In the transition period toward the end of the nineteenth century, the decorations range from blobs and daubs to very fine painting (Ill. 148). When judging the age of a piece, it is helpful to remember that there is a feeling of honesty about the porcelains made in the last part of the nineteenth century—even up to, say, 1915. If the work was good, it was very good, and anything missing could be attributed to lack of time. On the other hand, if the work was poor, it was the result of haste, and no pretense was made about it. This is the principal difference between wares made during this period and those made a short time later in the twenties. During this later period corners were cut to save time and costs; at first glance the wares appear to be of a much better quality than they actually are. Fine brushwork was replaced by a smear of paint outlined or highlighted with a few strokes of enamel. In the older pieces the enamel decoration was consistent throughout; if, for example, the flowers were very well done, then the leaves were equally well done. In the later versions, which are now unmarked, having been shipped with a paper sticker showing the country of origin, often the flowers were painted with care but the leaves were merely dabs of color with an outline to show the shape. In Ill. 149 the leaves on the coffeepot are outlined in gold and deep green, but the middle of the leaves consists only of dabs of green. On the vase in Ill. 150 the leaves have a few lines representing veins. Another tell-

tale indication of age is the lack of symmetry in the enamel decoration: On the older pieces this came as a natural result of the artist's work; in the later imitations it appears contrived.

Another characteristic of the older pieces is that very often something is missing from the design, no doubt through haste at the last moment, for generally the rest of the decoration has been done with great care. On the unmarked vase in Color Plate 6, there is a rosebud in the reserve on the front of the neck, but on the back the picture was never completed.

Symmetrical designs have the appearance of being symmetrical, but in actual fact are not (Ill. 151). This lack of symmetry gives the design a warmth and beauty that are the antithesis of the coldness of machine-made perfection. This human inperfection, however, should not be confused with deliberate deformation, which always appears false and contrived. Dr. Yanagi, in Bernard Leach's translation of various articles published in *The Unknown Craftsman* by Yanagi Sōetsu, speaks at length on the beauty of irregularity and on other aspects of beauty that we are fast losing sight of in our love affair with the machine.

As mass production increased, hand painting was superseded, or at least augmented, by decals. Many pieces are marked "hand painted" but in actual fact have a very small amount of hand painting on them. For example, on the Noritake dish in Ill. 152, only the colored line below the flower border is hand painted; the rest of the decoration was made with a decal. This was the method used for many of the cheap pre-World War II wares.

The decal was transferred to the glazed piece and any hand-painted work then added to the printed design, so that both could be fired at the same time. This was a very economical method of producing wares that could truthfully bear the legend "hand painted"; the company was not obliged to say exactly what was painted by hand.

Sometimes it is not easy to see what was

149. *This close-up of the teapot in Ill. 215 shows the method of outlining petals and leaves with a few hasty strokes, in contrast to the painstaking work shown in Ill. 147 and 148.*

150. *Ewer-vase (c. 1930) in the style of late nineteenth-century wares (see Color Plate 6). The brushwork is not as fine on this vase, and the handle was formed in the same mold as the rest of the piece, instead of being made separately and attached with slip.*

151. *Sugar and creamer (M-in-Wreath) are very well made of white porcelain, with small landscapes and gold border decoration. The landscapes are delicately painted with considerable detail in their miniature size, but the gold border is somewhat irregular, with an apparent intent to avoid constricting symmetry.*

152. Celery dish (Noritake, red M-in-Wreath mark) has stylized flowers, a gold edge, and openings at both ends to simulate handles. Although the backstamp reads "Hand painted," the only hand painting is the line around the center of the dish; the rest of the decoration was done with a decalcomania.

hand painted and what was not. In such a case it is best to examine two similar parts of the design and see whether the color misses the outline in both in exactly the same way. If it does, then the decoration is a decal.

Motifs:

Flowers and landscapes were the most popular decorations on the export wares of this period. Certain mythological creatures, human figures, and simple decorative patterns were also widely used.

Flowers: All kinds of flowers were portrayed: the rose, chrysanthemum, violet, iris, orchid, lotus, azalea, poppy, cornflower, plum blossom, cherry blossom, and so on (Ill. 154). On the older pieces, the shading of the background was as important as the actual motif; for instance, a soft gray was often used as a background for flowers in pastel shades.

Anyone wishing to make a collection of this type of Japanese export ware should study the Japanese way of painting roses on pieces of this date; familiarity with the style of the work can be of great help when deciding if an unmarked piece is of Japanese origin or not. The Japanese generally painted a rose with less petal detail than did the English or Germans of the same period. Look carefully at the Nippon Pagoda vase in Ill. 155, the unmarked teapot in Ill. 170, and the Pointed Crown chocolate pot in Ill. 176. I have purposely included this last piece because, although the brushwork is not of the same quality as that on the other two

mentioned, it is still in the same style. Roses were frequently portrayed in combination —a light pink one with a dark pink one.

The way in which flower sprays are arranged is another indication of Japanese origin. For an example of rose spray treatment, study the Maple Leaf celery dish in Ill. 156. In a piece of this nature, a long spray of roses on one side is balanced by a small nosegay of roses on the other side that is not centrally placed. The roses are in several colors, and the leaves in several shades of green; the whole design is artistically balanced both in form and color; to change one color in the roses would be to spoil the whole effect.

The Japanese concept that in nature there is balance but not symmetry is also illustrated in the design on the cover of the Kutani box in Ill. 76. No two nosegays are the same, and—even more interesting—the two with chrysanthemums are next to each other, instead of opposite, as they would have been had the piece been European instead of Japanese.

Certain flowers are symbols of the seasons. Daffodils and the crocuslike *Adonis amurensis* are for spring. The lily and the *shakuyaku*, or herbaceous peony (shown on the lace dish, Color Plate 1), represent summer. The lotus (water lily) is for autumn and the crimson plum for winter. The deer with maple leaves is another symbol for autumn. (See the Kutani chocolate set in Color Plate 11 for a description of this type of decoration.)

Chrysanthemums are said to promote good health and longevity; the Imperial

153. The three Kutani-style pieces are decorated with human figures. The small bowl at left with attached saucer carries a green T-in-Plum-Blossom mark and "Japan." The sugar bowl, which has Mt. Fuji on the other side, bears the green Pagoda Nippon mark, and the jar is marked with Japanese characters reading Kutani on a red brushstroke. These three pieces are similar in coloring, the figures being dressed in red, lilac, and blue. The two Nippon plates with similar decoration have considerable white enamel beading and gold. The one at left, with roses in two shades of pink, bears the M-in-Wreath mark. The one at right, decorated with violets, carries the Maple Leaf mark.

154. *Examples of Nippon floral decoration. The dish with handles has purple and yellow chrysanthemums, not centered. The sugar bowl and creamer are embellished with pink roses; the friendship cup and saucer, with violets. On the three-footed dish are cornflowers outlined in gold against a green band. All are well made, and all are marked M-in-Wreath except the footed dish, which bears the t"t" symbol.*

155. *Nippon vase, H. 10″, has Pagoda mark in blue. The brushwork on this piece is not of such good quality as, for example, that on the chocolate cups (green Pagoda mark) in Ill. 180.*

156. Celery dish (Nippon, Maple Leaf mark) with tasteful decoration.

chrysanthemum, emblem of the Imperial family, has sixteen petals. The blue bell-flower *(kikyo)*, an autumn flower, is often used as a contrasting color in a floral spray, particularly by Noritake. Various kinds of nuts are used for decoration, the browns giving much warmth to the design (Ill. 157).

Birds of all kinds are used, either alone or as part of a scene. Certain birds and flowers are often used together. The sparrow and bamboo are shown together on the cup and saucer in Ill. 158, and a dove and plum combination is portrayed on the coffee set in Ill. 159. These associations, along with the quail and millet, the swallow and willow, all probably stem from Chinese sources. The orange and cuckoo, the plum and nightingale, however, are from native Japanese sources.

Mythological Creatures: The Hō-ō bird is another popular decoration that has been used for centuries on ceramic wares (Ill. 160). The Hō-ō is something between a bird of paradise and a phoenix. The word is often translated as "phoenix," but this is not really correct, as the creature does not have the attributes of the phoenix.

Dragons were also frequently used as a

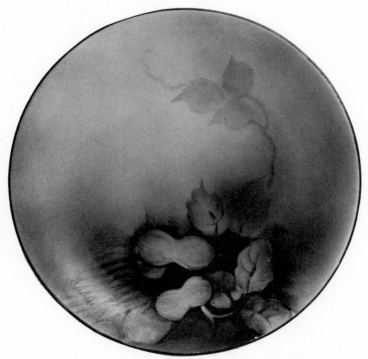

157. Plate with Noritake M-in-Wreath, green mark. The motifs are in autumn shades ranging from red brown through golden brown. Mr. and Mrs. T. M. Lotito

158. *Small cup and saucer with "sparrow and bamboo" decoration. Both pieces bear Japanese characters reading "Imura Company at Yokohama, Japan." They are very well made, probably late nineteenth century.*

159. *Coffeepot, sugar, and creamer have colorful dove and plum decoration. Probably c. 1930, but unmarked. The raised star under each piece, unglazed, served as support during firing.*

160. *Cups and saucers with Hō-ō bird design in gold and a yellow border. The cherry blossom has a red center, which gives an attractive touch of color. Noritake, red M-in-Wreath. Mr. and Mrs. T. M. Lotito*

161. *Dish, Occupied Japan, has Chinese-style decoration with a dragon (five-clawed, Chinese style) and the Hō-ō bird.*

162. *Satsuma-style incense burner (koro), c. 1920, with three* shishi *dogs; the one on the top holds a ball* (tama), *the jewel of omniscience. Unmarked.*

decorative device on ceramics. They were supposed to inhabit the sky, and the Hō-ō bird the earth (Ill. 161). The Chinese dragon is depicted with five claws, and the Japanese with three.

The *shishi* dog is something between a lion and a dog. Portrayed in pairs, *shishi* keep evil away; when shown singly the *shishi* is pictured with a ball *(tama)*, the jewel of omniscience. Note the Satsuma-style incense burner in Ill. 162. The *shishi* dog is shown on the cover with the ball; the two on the sides are a pair. In pairs, one dog often has its mouth open and the other has it closed. The openmouthed dog is female; the one with the mouth closed is the male.

Landscapes: All kinds of landscapes, and especially lake scenes, are found on all classes of post-1868 export wares. These are not the Chinese-style landscapes with craggy mountains, but true pictures of the Japanese countryside. In my personal opinion, the pieces with landscape scenes are the finest of these wares. They were doubtless inspired by European pieces of a similar nature, but there is a marked difference between the two. On European pieces generally the scenery is a background for figures, animals, or birds, but on the Japanese pieces the scenery is the all-important thing. On a good piece the painting is very fine—the decorator must have taken infinite pains with his picture (Ill. 163). Unfortunately, the

163. At left is a detail photograph of the Nippon M-in-Wreath vase from Color Plate 10. The detail photograph at right shows another Nippon M-in-Wreath vase with good brushwork. Cows drinking in the stream are the central theme, but a peasant in his straw raincoat watches them in the fading light.

fine pieces were produced during a very short period, and the quality of the work deteriorated rapidly when decorators became unable to spend the requisite amount of time on a single piece. Collectors should take good care of the fine pieces they have; they are not likely to be made again.

Sunsets were frequently depicted. Japan has a moist climate, and in consequence has spectacular sunsets. But the Japanese appreciate a rainy day, and prefer natural beauty in rain or mist. This may seem strange to us, who prefer to go out in the sunshine rather than getting wet in the rain, but to the Japanese a landscape can be infinitely more beautiful in the rain than in the sunshine. Bright sunshine dazzles the eyes, and forms and colors become indistinct, whereas a light rain or mist brings out the contours of the land, and shapes and colors are apparent that would otherwise blend

into a flat background on a bright sunny day. The Japanese call a rainy day a masculine day and a sunny one a feminine day.

Landscapes are pictured in different ways (Ill. 164). Some sets have parts of a single landscape on each piece so that, placed side by side, they form one whole picture. Generally a landscape on a vase goes all the way around, with no start or finish, although there is always much less detail on the back. The Japanese like to picture scenes as though glimpsed from some special vantage point, again their love of obscurity rather than the obvious. On the small pitcher in Ill. 165, we seem to be standing in a grape arbor and looking through the vines at a scene of Japanese ladies in the distance. On the vase in Ill. 155, we appear to be looking from behind a rosebush toward the mountains.

Figures: Generally the figures por-

164. On the Noritake dresser set (Tree Crest mark), the landscape is depicted in a different way on each piece. This is not one of the better Noritake sets, as the colors are too strong and garish —the hills are deep purple, the roofs too red, and the yellow bridge does not blend well. The brushwork is also poor. The pieces in the other group are all Nippon with quite restrained gold decoration.

165. The four pieces grouped together all have Kaga-style decoration featuring scenes with ladies. The creamer at the right of the group has an underglaze blue border; the other three pieces, red overglaze enamel. The small covered box is unmarked, but the others are Nippon with the Torii mark. The pitcher (left) shown by itself, also Kaga style, shows the figures as if glimpsed through a grape arbor. The sugar and creamer set in the third photograph ("Made in Japan" with the Torii mark) has underglaze blue borders and a scene with a boy carrying baskets.

trayed on these export porcelains represent a type of person (lady, man, child), rather than individuals (Ill. 165). The exception is on Satsuma wares, where the figures look like real people rather than types (Ill. 89 and Color Plate 15). The impersonal figures are usually part of a landscape instead of being the central theme, as on European pieces. Even the peasant in his straw raincoat (see Ill. 163) is part of the scenery, far less important than his cows. This is an interesting concept and a true one: One individual man is insignificant compared to the wonders of nature.

Figures used in other ways are shown in a set on which the Immortal Poets are portrayed (Ill. 78). Chinese men are depicted on the Satsuma-style plate in Ill. 86 and one of the cups in Color Plate 9. A sugar bowl and creamer in Ill. 165 have a boy carrying a basket. Pieces marked Occupied Japan sometimes also have portraits on them.

Some wares have Chinese-style decoration. The vase in Ill. 169 has a Chinese-style landscape with birds. In Color Plate 1 a covered vegetable dish with decoration is reminiscent of Chinese rose medallion, and in Color Plate 2 a Nippon bowl has a Chinese-style bird and blossom decoration. The latter type of decoration can also be found in later wares—Ill. 222 shows a Made in Japan piece, and in Ill. 229 a similar design is marked Occupied Japan.

Decorative Patterns: Such patterns are carried out in colored enamels or in heavy gold (Ills. 164 & 166). They are never perfectly symmetrical, although they may appear to be so at first glance. Cloisonné effects are freely used, either as border decorations (Ill. 167) or as the principal motif (Color Plate 16).

Of course, many other types of decora-

166. *The close-up of a cup shows a decorative enamel border design that appears to be symmetrical, but is not. Mark is Nippon, M-in-Wreath.* Mr. and Mrs. H. Edward Anderson. *The syrup pot shown in close-up is the same one that appears in Color Plate 17.*

167. On the Nippon M-in-Wreath vase is depicted a Middle East scene with camels, palm trees, and mountains, and a cloisonné-effect border. The small Nippon mustard pot (Rising Sun mark) appears to present a palm tree growing out of pyramids.

tion were used as well. Middle East scenes were popular, and they are the most amusing to study, as quite often the decorator relied largely on his imagination. The M-in-Wreath vase in Ill. 167 has a credible picture on it, but on the Rising Sun mustard pot in Ill. 167 a palm tree appears to be growing in the middle of a pyramid!

Oddments of decoration turn up all the time. For example, on the vase in Ill. 168 is the picture of an ancient carriage with a lady's sleeves hanging out, and the cookie jar in Ill. 168 shows a tearoom. This type of decoration is generally later than Nippon; most of it dates between the two world wars.

168. Two pieces from the 1921–1939 period. The vase shows an ancient carriage with the lady occupant's sleeves hanging through the doors in front. The cookie jar bears a scene featuring a tearoom. Both are unmarked pieces.

14

Pre-Nippon Porcelain Wares (1868-1890)

169. Octagonal vase, h. 12", has Chinese-style decoration in overglaze blue. Late nineteenth century. Unmarked.

This chapter will discuss the pieces that are the forerunners of the Nippon wares. They either have no mark at all or bear a potter's name. They are export wares of a transition period, influenced by the West in form and decoration, but still retaining much of their oriental heritage.

These pieces are generally characterized by artistic merit and good workmanship. They are the most individual of all the ceramic export wares of the entire period, being the potter's own adaptation of the new style. Each piece has something striking about it, either in form or color.

The body is made of good quality porcelain. The earliest of these wares were made in Arita, but Seto soon followed the lead, and by the mid-seventies both areas were producing large quantities of the new type of wares. Decoration was done locally to start with, but within a few years wares were sent to Tokyo for decoration.

In this period the vast impersonality of mass production had not yet been reached, and we can still sense the potter's hand and thoughts in his work, although at times there is evidence of a rush to finish. No doubt the agent was due to arrive shortly to collect the completed pieces. Throughout this period the wares were made by families or small groups of potters, and as most kilns produced porcelain at one time or another, a great deal of porcelain was made.

170. The unmarked late nineteenth-century tea set has underglaze blue borders and handles decorated with an intricate gold pattern. The roses are in two shades of pink. On this set the lids fit over the openings, in contrast to the lid on the separate teapot pictured in close-up, which sets down into the opening. This teapot, also unmarked and late nineteenth century, is an example of the Japanese predilection for odd numbers: it has five feet (three in front, two in back), five gold flowers on the front, three on the back; the gold flowers on the lid are in two sets of three. There is a great deal of coralene beading in intricate gold tracery over the light and dark pink roses. Lid and body are unglazed where they meet, probably so that both could be fired together. Note the stubby spout and Q-shaped handle.

The body of pre-Nippon pieces is generally very well made, with no trace of where the mold joined. Handles, spouts, and other parts were attached with great care and smoothed to make a neat join. The shapes have a distinct oriental feeling inter-mixed with their new occidental form, especially in the handles and spouts. In most pieces the Eastern heritage is stronger than the Western influence, as is evidenced by the irregularity the Japanese love in shape and design (see the lace dish, Color Plate 1), and the use of odd numbers like three, five, and seven in the decoration on the teapot in Ill. 170.

The decoration is not generally placed exactly in the center. This is an important point to remember when examining a piece for country of origin. But remember that this is a general rule; it must be considered in conjunction with other things, as there are exceptions all around.

Fluting is much in evidence on all kinds of pieces, and it is another mark of this transition period. Cups and saucers are paper-thin (a speciality of Seto) and very often fluted. These pieces were all made before the introduction of the jigger, and drain molds and solid casting molds lent themselves well to fluting. Even the base of a chocolate pot could be elaborately fluted (see Color Plate 7).

Pieces of this period with a cover or lid were often left unglazed on both cover and body where the two meet. These unglazed areas are important to look for when trying to decide if a piece is of this period or a later imitation. Later pieces are likely to be glazed on these spots.

Lids for teapots, sugar bowls, and the like were made in two styles: so that they fit either over the opening of the pot or down into it (Ill. 170). Lids of the latter type always seem rather small for the openings they cover. This type was also used for Kutani wares (Ill. 80) and for some Nippon.

Finials, mostly very elaborate, were usually made separately from the lid. They were attached when leather-hard, as were the knobs.

The handles on these pre-Nippon pieces retained much of their Japanese style, and

Fig. 4. The main types of handles used on pre-Nippon porcelain wares. Top, left to right: *Plain round handle, generally used on teapots, sugar bowls, and creamers; the same type of substantial handle but used for taller pieces (e.g., chocolate pots); a simple pointed handle used for teapots, sugar bowls, creamers, and other pieces, and—in a finer form—on Kutani wares of the same period. The first two types were often in underglaze blue and had elaborate gold designs painted on them.* Bottom, left to right: *Q-shaped pointed handle; plain cup handle; the very popular bamboo-style handle, used on all types of pieces and also on later wares.*

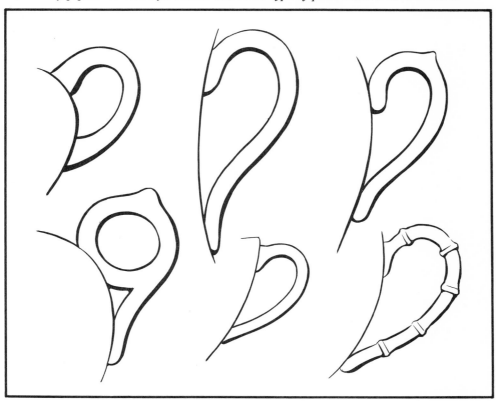

Fig. 5. *Pre-Nippon spouts and feet. Spouts were generally rather short and pointed, and often did not pour well. A great many pieces were footed. The usual kind of foot was curved, either solid (bottom right) for smaller pieces—e.g., tea sets—or made in a drain mold (bottom left) for larger pieces—e.g., vases. Those made in a drain mold had a small hole on the inside, which allowed the steam to escape while the piece was being fired, so that the foot would not explode.*

were generally substantial and strong. Fig. 4 shows the main types of handles used. Those on teapots and chocolate pots were often in underglaze blue with elaborate designs painted on them. There was plenty of room on these broad handles for even a chrysanthemum design. The plainness of the style was often counteracted by more intricate work where the handle and body joined, as on the vase in Color Plate 6, which has oriental-looking supports at the top, and on the chocolate pot (Color Plate 7) with a ribbon applied handle. Handles of this type are quite indicative of the age of a piece, as later imitations tended to become overelaborate and clumsy.

The spouts were also very characteristic of the period, being generally rather short and pointed (Fig. 5). Very often they do not pour too well. Many of the teapots made between the 1870s and 1900 make far better ornaments for the china cabinet than vehicles for tea making. The potters do not seem to have understood the Western teapot very well; Japanese teapots are of another type.

A great many pieces were footed. The usual kind of foot was curved, solid for smaller pieces and hollow for larger ones (Fig. 5). In both cases the feet were attached to the body with slip after both parts were leather-hard.

Vases are in a class of their own, unique in their mixed heritage of East and West,

and very attractive. Ornamental vases had no place in the Japanese home—that type was made entirely for export. A vase for the Japanese home is intended to hold flowers and to be unobtrusive so that the flowers show to their best advantage. Export vases, on the other hand, were not intended to hold flowers; indeed, putting flowers in them is a mistake, as it spoils the line. The white flared opening at the top is a necessary part of the design. It provides both balance in form and color contrast to the enameled decoration on the body. When flowers are placed in such a vase, this is all lost (Ill. 171).

Characteristic of this period was the large amount of painstaking handwork used. Not only was the decoration painted very delicately with great attention to detail, but the biscuit was given considerable attention after coming out of the mold. Generally there is no trace at all of where the mold joined. As many of these pieces were made in one place, in contrast to pieces later sent away for decoration, the biscuit and enamel decoration are much more homogeneous than in most later pieces. The coralene beading was applied with the painted design in mind; it was an integral part of the decoration, rather than a decorative border as on the later Nippon pieces.

On pre-Nippon wares, often there were as many as four different kinds of coralene beading and patterns on a single piece, and generally that on the front was different from that on the back. On some pieces coralene beading was the major part of the decoration, overshadowing the enamel design, as on the teapot in Ill. 170.

Coralene beading is an important help when estimating the age of a piece. Generally speaking, if a piece has an assortment of coralene beading varying both in the size of the dots and the complexity of the pattern, it can be assumed to be from this period and not a later imitation. Shortcuts that were supposed to give the impression of complex work are a sure indication of a later era.

Coralene beading on a small piece like a cup is a strong indication that the piece belongs to the pre-Nippon era (Ill. 171).

There was much more use of solid colors on pre-Nippon pieces than on later Nippon, particularly the various shades of turquoise, ranging from almost blue to almost green. One wonders if they liked it the best of the new European-style enamels; it does show off most other colors to their greatest advantage. A deep red was also used frequently.

The enamel decoration was painstakingly done all over a piece, everything done equally well, the leaves as well as the flowers. Blobs of color with an outline to show the shape are the mark of a later period (again, a method of cutting corners and eliminating costs and work).

A smaller range of flower varieties was used on these pieces than on the later Nippon. Roses and chrysanthemums were the most frequently used flowers, although flowers native to Japan were also depicted at times. The *shakuyaku,* or pink herbaceous peony, symbol of summer, was used as decoration on the lace dish in Color Plate 1, the blue *kikyo,* or bellflower (an autumn flower), appears on the covered vegetable dish in the same color plate.

Usually the floral designs on the front and back of a piece were different, the one on the back having fewer flowers and the colors being arranged differently. On some pieces the enamel background of the floral design was painted in a different color on the back. On the chocolate pot in Color Plate 7 the background on the front was done in gold, but on the back a light turquoise was used. However, the background of the flowers on the footed vase in Color Plate 6 was painted in the same color front and back, but the pattern of the surrounding coralene beading decoration was simplified on the back.

Gold was freely used on these wares, and elaborate gold designs were painted on the underglaze blue. This blue was done with imported cobalt oxide.

Cobalt oxide, as already explained, is much easier to use than the native cobalt, and can be applied in a perfectly uniform manner, but unfortunately art and perfection are incompatible. The artist strives for perfection, but it is the minute imperfections that give warmth and beauty. This is why meticulous handwork has a beauty that no machine-made article can have. In these pre-Nippon wares, as well as in some Nippon wares, there is still much of this kind of beauty that was lost when the machine took over.

Many cups had the more important pattern painted on the inside, and when this was done the inside of the cup was smoothed very carefully. This decoration is seen frequently on older wares, but it can also be found on later wares, especially those marked Occupied Japan.

Unusual pieces can be found throughout the post-1868 period, and many require study to ascertain if they are Japanese or not. The covered vegetable dish in Color Plate 1 is a good example, for on cursory inspection it looks Chinese. However, besides having a Japanese potter's name on the underside, it is decorated with men wearing Japanese clothing, and there are also many Japanese-style irregularities in the decoration, as well as a difference in the coloring. The Japanese use more vivid shades, and the brightness of the pink is particularly obvious. There are also unglazed portions where cover and body meet.

Condensed milk jars were made in this period as well as later (Color Plate 9). The finger hole at the bottom was put there so that the empty can could be pushed up, but there was no hole in the lid for a spoon— each person was expected to use his own. A jam or jelly pot had no hole in the bottom, but there was one in the lid for a spoon.

171. Two late nineteenth-century pieces with a considerable amount of coralene beading. Mr. and Mrs. T. M. Lotito

15

Nippon Wares (1891-1921)

The name Nippon began to appear on Japanese wares in 1891, after the McKinley Tariff Act was passed in October 1890. This act stated, among other things, that articles imported into the United States from abroad must be marked with the name of the country of origin written in English. The Japanese used their own name for their country, "Nippon," and wares from Japan imported into this country bore that name for thirty years. However, in 1921 the United States Treasury decreed that "Japan" must be used instead of "Nippon," as the latter was a Japanese word.

These wares bear a wide range of other marks, but unfortunately, except as a general form of classification, the marks are of very little use to the collector. For the most part they were either the identification marks of agents in Japan or the marks of importers abroad. The agents made arrangements for pieces to be sent "in the white" from the factories where they were made to decorators in various places, and then returned to the agents for export. This is why the marks have very little meaning, except as a means of dating the pieces. An agent might get blanks from a number of different factories and ship them to a group of decorators; since there were whole communities of decorators, each piece in a batch of identical wares from one factory might pass through the hands of a different decorator. Conversely, the same decorator might work on wares from a number of different factories,

or from different agents, and he might get them mixed up (Ill. 172).

Symbols were used as identification marks because they were the easiest thing. Japanese potters could not read English, and the foreign agents and importers did not read Japanese, but everyone could understand a symbol.

Of course, the marks do provide some information for the collector, although it is of a limited nature. For example, the various agents and importers naturally had their own preferences, so there is some similarity of style and quality in the wares each one dealt with. Location was another factor. Porcelain, for instance, made in the Seto area and decorated in the vicinity was much whiter than that made in factories in the Kaga area and decorated in that style (Ill. 173).

Great changes took place during this period (1891–1921) as mass production increased; wares produced from 1915 to 1921 were generally very different from those made in the early Nippon days around the turn of the century. In 1900 production was still mainly by small groups or families, but by 1920 numerous companies had been formed, some quite small and some much larger. The early Nippon wares were almost as individual as those in the preceding period, but by about 1915 the same shapes were repeated again and again, although with different decoration and often bearing different marks (Ill. 174).

149

172. Although these Nippon plates with pink roses were obviously decorated as a set, the Nippon marks on the backs are not the same. The top center one has the cherry-blossom Nippon mark, but the others are marked T-in-Wreath.

173. Kaga-style Nippon ware chocolate set; Torii mark. Decoration of this type was done mainly by decalcomania, with a few added dabs of overglaze enamel color. Any gold was applied directly over the glaze, never over the enamel decoration. Gray porcelain.

174. Nippon mayonnaise set. Although this set carries the Square Crown mark, identically shaped pieces with similar decoration can be found in all the Nippon marks. Mayonnaise sets marked Noritake are slightly smaller.

When studying these wares, both the quality of the porcelain and the decoration have to be taken into account. Good quality bodies did not necessarily get correspondingly good decoration, and some poor quality bodies got better decoration than it would seem they deserved. The decoration ranged from fine work, as on the M-in-Wreath vase in Ill. 163, to the blobs and dabs of the Torii pieces (Ill. 173). Pieces made toward the end of the period usually did not have the fine brushwork of the earlier pieces, and later copies of the earlier pieces are interesting to compare (Ill. 175).

When it comes to trying to date a piece of this period, even though we know the general trend of increased mass production, dating is often a difficult task. As a general rule one may assume that if a piece has a look of mixed East and West heritage, it is from the early Nippon period. Coralene beading similar to that on pre-Nippon pieces is also characteristic of the early days of Nippon, and the use of groups of daisylike chrysanthemums, another popular decoration, may indicate an early piece of Nippon.

As the Nippon period progressed, the same type of molds was used again and

175. The plate at the top (Nippon Maple Leaf mark) must have been a copy of the set below (Nippon M-in-Wreath mark). The coloring is similar, but there is much less detail on the plate—for example, the boat on the plate is outlined with a few strokes, but on the dish it is painted with considerable detail. Pyramids have been added to the picture on the plate.

176. The chocolate set bears the Rising Sun mark. Miss Veronica Kiley. *The separate chocolate pot has the Pointed Crown mark. The Rising Sun set is of far better quality than the Pointed Crown pot—the porcelain is sparkling white; the floral decoration is well painted, as is the delicate cross-hatching in gold on the border. The Rising Sun pot is much better made also; the finial was molded separately, in contrast to the Pointed Crown pot, which had the finial included in the mold for the lid. The finial and handle of the Pointed Crown pot have a blurred, clumsy appearance. Most Nippon chocolate sets were made with five cups and saucers only, in Japanese style. Later sets had six.*

again, but the most commercial development was in the use of the jigger. This took over gradually during the middle of the Nippon period; by the end of that period the jigger was in general use for making plates, saucers, cups, bowls, and the like. The manufacture of the ten-inch plate presented the greatest problem, and plates of this size made on a jigger date from the late Nippon period. During the early Nippon period large plates were made in solid casting molds.

The use of the jigger was a great boon to ceramics manufacturers because they could make their wares much faster, but it was very unfortunate for the collector. A piece made on a jigger has perfection but less beauty than a similar piece made by pouring.

The shapes of Nippon period pieces are generally Western, although they have an oriental touch. Good pieces have a lighter and more graceful form than comparable English or German pieces, both of which have more of a sturdy good-sense approach. Pieces made in the Nippon period usually had the handles, finials, or knobs made separately and, when hard, attached to the body with slip. Late in the period the molds began to include handles and similar attachments, although this did not become a general practice until the 1920s.

The most characteristic wares of the Nippon period are the chocolate sets, which carry many different Nippon marks. The molds used were almost identical—only the handles and finials varied slightly—but the quality of the porcelain was variable. It ranged from a very fine white, as in pieces with the Rising Sun mark, to a poor-quality gray. The two chocolate pots in Ill. 176 also show how the ornaments on the handle originally served as strategically placed supports, but after much repetition the original purpose was lost and the ornaments served no purpose.

Handles eventually became mostly Westernized, although there was still a touch of the Orient on many of them. Feet very often were merely a small ball of clay (Ill. 177).

The important characteristics of the pre-Nippon group were their general shape, the use of solid color, and the extensive use of coralene beading. Nippon wares are remarkable for fine painting, particularly of landscape scenes that go entirely around the pieces, and of a vast array of floral decoration. These wares are often not only real works of art, but a labor of love—the time spent painting them must have been out of all proportion to the monetary recompense.

Elaborate coralene beading of the type

177. Mayonnaise bowl and ladle; M-in-Wreath. Mr. and Mrs. H. Edward Anderson.

178. *Two plates, c. 1920. The plate on the left, with the swan, carries a mark saying both "Nippon" and "Made in Japan." The one on the right reads "Made in Nippon." The coralene beading on the swan plate was made with very fine dots of slip, but the rose-decorated plate has beading made with drops of white enamel.*

used on pre-Nippon wares is rare; a cheaper form superseded it on Nippon wares. Instead of being made with dots of slip, a fine beading was made with dots of enamel painted over in gold. On some older pieces of Nippon it is possible to find both kinds on a single piece. An even cheaper method of producing a beaded line was to make it with enameled dots in a contrasting color (Ill. 178). However, the disappearance of dots of slip for coralene beading was not caused altogether by reasons of economy, but rather on account of mass production. A piece would have to be designed and completed in one place if the coralene beading was to form part of, and complement, the enamel decoration. If the piece was to be shipped out as a blank to be decorated elsewhere, the coralene beading could be applied only as a border decoration, for example, in conjunction with underglaze blue, which was applied before the biscuit firing. (Incidentally, coralene beading decorated in gold makes a very neat edge to an underglaze blue border.) If the decorator wished to use coralene beading as part of his design, he was obliged to apply it as raised dots of enamel, then paint it with gold (Ill. 179). This last coat of gold, of course, had to have a separate firing at a lower temperature after the other enamels were fired, so if the decorator did not cover the enamel dots with gold, a firing was saved.

As already mentioned, the quality of the porcelain varied considerably. The finest and whitest can be found on pieces bearing the Rising Sun symbol—in fact, Rising Sun pieces are notable for their consistently excellent-quality bodies. Pieces with the Maple Leaf mark are usually of good quality, as are those with the M-in-Wreath. Wares marked with the Pagoda are variable, from excellent to mediocre; the mark was applied in more than one color, according to quality—in

179. *Ornamental vase, M-in-Wreath, h. 11", is embellished with flesh-colored roses framed in basket-weave motif. The beading on this piece was first made with dots of enamel, then painted with gold.*

180. The chocolate cups and saucers and nut dish (green Pagoda mark) show fine decorative work. The underglaze blue is patterned with gold; the roses are in two shades of pink.

green, blue, and magenta, in that order (Ill. 180). The Imperial, Torii, and both Crown marks generally appear on grayer bodies (Ill. 181).

It should be pointed out that, as far as decoration was concerned, the decorators often made the most of a gray body by using it as a soft background for a pastel design; in fact, very often more gray was added to create a beautiful shaded background. White is not the best background for colors, since it creates too much contrast. On the other hand, Rising Sun wares glory in their pure white body and glaze, and use floral decoration of a restrained pastel shade as a foil to the sparkling whiteness (Ill. 182).

In speaking of the different Nippon marks, it should be explained that the M-in-Wreath pieces are included here, rather than in the Noritake chapter where they rightfully belong, for several reasons. One reason is that many people do not know M-in-Wreath pieces were made by the Noritake Company, and so they will look for them in this chapter. I feel that they should be included with the rest of the Nippon wares rather than with the Noritake, as they possess so many characteristics of the other Nippon pieces. Unfortunately, the Noritake Company records were destroyed during the war, and as there is very little informa-

tion available about the company, I have not been able to discover a satisfying explanation as to why the name Noritake was omitted from these wares. The "M" in the wreath decoration stands, of course, for the Morimura Brothers in New York, the sole importers of Noritake.

Frankly, I am puzzled at the difference between the bodies of the pieces bearing the Noritake mark and of those with only the M-in-Wreath. The Noritake pieces are of a consistent good quality; their dimensions are slightly different from those of the other Nippon wares, but, on the other hand, the bodies of the M-in-Wreath pieces are of variable quality, and they are of the same dimensions as the other Nippon wares. Since the decoration is always of high quality, I surmise that, in order to fulfill their large export quota, the Noritake Company decorated blanks from other companies and exported them under the M-in-Wreath mark, but without the Noritake name. This is only a suggestion, and to counter it I must point out that Noritake made blanks to be sent out for decoration and exported under other marks. Blanks bearing the M-in-Wreath mark were also exported for decoration elsewhere (Ill. 183).

Two other Noritake marks were used on Nippon wares without the Noritake

181. *The small dish with handles has the Square Crown mark. This is an unusual and attractive piece, but the porcelain body is rather gray. The round bowl, which has the Pointed Crown mark, is a poor quality piece with a heavy gray body and inferior brushwork.*

182. *An assortment of wares with the Rising Sun mark. These pieces are characterized by a sparkling white body and restrained tasteful decoration.*

183. Jam pot marked M-in-Wreath. This must have been exported to a studio abroad for decoration—the signature "W. Rose" appears below the smaller rose. The decoration is not in Japanese style, neither in brushwork nor colors.

184. Octagonal dish, R. C. Nippon mark. An elegant piece in restrained muted colors.

name. They were the R. C. mark (Ill. 184) and the Tree Crest mark (see Chapter 16). The R. C. mark was used on good quality pieces that usually had a restrained style of decoration. Wares bearing the Tree Crest mark were usually decorated with a heavy gold border.

In the Nippon period gold was used plentifully, especially on wares with the Maple Leaf symbol (Color Plate 11 and Ill. 185). Pieces bearing this mark were the most flamboyant of all the Nippon wares, the shapes often quite unusual, although many apparently were made in the same molds as pieces

bearing other marks. These wares, like the M-in-Wreath wares, came from the Nagoya area, and there is a close relationship between the two.

There are many different Nippon marks, probably more than sixty. They can be found on a wide variety of pieces, ranging from fine ornamental ones to some very mediocre wares. However, among these there are many fine pieces for everyday use (Ill. 186). I feel that in their way they correspond to the *getomono* Dr. Yanagi talked about. Although he was speaking of unassuming and sturdy pottery wares made for

185. *The vase, h. 9", bears the Maple Leaf mark. The flowers, leaves, and stems are all outlined in gold. The base is attached with a screw. The sugar and creamer, with t"t" mark, have finely detailed gold decoration highlighted with turquoise blue enamel. The bowl on stand (two pieces) has the M-in-Wreath mark. The black border is heavily decorated with gold; there is a landscape inside the bowl. Notice the interesting handles and feet. Mr. and Mrs. Henry J. Holst*

186. *Three attractive Nippon pieces for every-day use. The celery dish bears azaleas with a border of intertwined leaves. Rising Sun mark. The octagonal dish, Imperial mark; the plate, M-in-Wreath mark. The decoration on the Rising Sun dish is set off by the sparkling whiteness of the body and glaze; on the other two pieces the backgrounds are in delicate shades of green and gray, which blend harmoniously with the floral decorations.*

hard usage, whose beauty lay in their combination of aesthetic appeal and practicality, it seems to me that the same quality exists in some of these export wares. They are in decorated porcelain, but they were intended for Westerners who used decorated porcelains as everyday wares. In these pieces there is the same anonymity of craftsmen who were unconcerned with fame, but who decorated the blanks they were given in very beautiful ways. The blanks were often made very tastefully, with elegant fluting and molding, and the decorator added to it, for example, a beautifully arranged sprig of flowers in delicate colors. Pieces of this nature are essentially ones to be enjoyed while they are being used.

Pieces bearing the Torii mark were direct descendants of Kaga *aka-e*, the red Kaga wares (see Chapter 7). The bodies were made from a course gray porcelain, and the decoration consisted mainly of a decalcomania of a landscape with figures, with added dabs of red, green, blue, and yellow enamel (Ill. 187). Generally a little gold was applied, and as it was always on a glazed area and never over enamel, it could be fired at the same time as the enamels. At times yellow enamel was substituted for gold, and this could be applied over the other enamels

and fired with them, instead of needing a separate firing as would have been necessary with gold. These wares were produced very fast and the decoration done on an assembly-line basis—one decorator painted the red, another the green, and so on. Their technique seems to have been hit or miss, and as often as not it was miss. However, inaccurate as these dashes of color were, the pieces still have a certain charm and warmth to them.

Not all Torii pieces were decorated with decalcomanias, although the majority of pieces were. Some pieces had their enamel decoration painted entirely by hand (Ill. 188). Collectors of moderate means can find plenty of variety and interest in Nippon wares (Ill. 189). The landscape vases are the more expensive items, although, of course, the ones made around 1920 were generally not as good as the earlier ones. The Egyptian scenes are very amusing and can be found on all kinds of pieces (Ill. 190). I have included an illustration of three different views of Mt. Fuji (Ill. 191), and for a modest financial outlay a very interesting collection of this nature could be formed. Nippon dolls may also be found, as well as wall plaques (Ill. 192). Among late Nippon wares are quite a good many copies of popular European styles—of

187. *A popular Torii design. Like many other Torii designs, this one can be found on both Nippon and Made in Japan wares.*

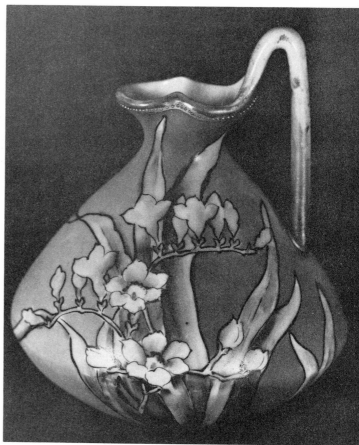

188. *A less usual type of Torii decoration. It is entirely hand painted, in contrast to the frequent use of decalcomania and dabs of paint.*

189. *Two M-in-Wreath pieces: A well-made pitcher of unusual shape with coralene beading decorated in gold; and a small bowl with white flowers.* Mr. and Mrs. T. M. Lotito

190. *Three M-in-Wreath pieces decorated with land-scapes. Plate at left, d. 10", shows a Japanese landscape in black and gold. Pinney Collection. Coaster, d. 3½", has a Dutch scene with windmill. Catharine Lotito. Plate at right has an Egyptian scene.*

191. *Views of Mt. Fuji. This type of decoration can be found on pieces marked with the Torii symbol and "Nippon" or "Japan," as well as "Made in Japan."*

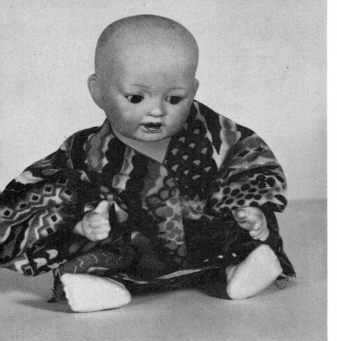

192. Collectible pieces found on the market today range from this appealing doll (incised "Nippon") to the rather grotesque wall plaque marked M-in-Wreath, which has holes on the back for hanging.

the Royal Bayreuth Rose Tapestry line and of Royal Doulton pieces, to name only two.

Many Nippon pieces were not marked. For example, certain pieces of a set might be marked and the rest unmarked, and so once the set is broken up, the unmarked pieces become unknown quantities. Often only one of a pair of vases would be marked. This situation creates problems in both dating and establishing country of origin. Wares of the Japanese export period are usually not too hard to place, however, if the overall feel of the porcelain is taken into account, as well as the combination of colors and general irregularity.

On Nippon ware, as has been pointed out, decorations that appear symmetrical are never quite that way, although sometimes this is hard to detect. A decoration can be symmetrically designed but unevenly spaced, and not symmetrical at all although it has that appearance (Ill. 193). In my opinion this lack of regularity is the most important thing to look for, and it is always there —perhaps only in the form of two colors reversed or some other slight change.

The question of date is a little more difficult. A piece may be an older one or it may be a copy. In general, more shortcuts were taken as time went by, and these became particularly noticeable as the Nippon period progressed.

193. *M-in-Wreath pieces: The two plates have pink and white roses in reserves and a gold border with coralene beading. Although these plates are part of a set, the central designs are not identical—the one on the right is much larger. In the group of three dishes the shamrock design on the celery dish appears symmetrical, but actually it is not. The covered creamer has a naturalistic floral border. Mr. and Mrs. T. M. Lotito. On the single plate, d. 10½", the rose design has been repeated with attention to regularity, but the border is quite uneven. On the Maple Leaf celery dish with gold border and pink roses, the alternating groups of roses are not the same on both sides—the larger groups are opposite the smaller groups.* Mr. and Mrs. T. M. Lotito

16

Noritake Wares

The Noritake Company, Ltd., was founded in Japan for the exclusive purpose of manufacturing chinawares for export. The company began in a small way early in the Meiji era, when the Morimura brothers established an office in New York in 1876, and a short time later another one in Nagoya. These offices handled the import-export formalities for chinawares made by several small factories in Japan and sold in the United States.

In 1904 the Noritake factory was established in Nagoya; in Japan it was called Nippon Toki Kabushiki Kaisha. The factory housed everything necessary for the making of chinaware: a gypsum shop produced plaster of Paris for the molds; the latest equipment was installed for preparing the clay and making the bodies; facilities for the decoration of the wares were designed on Western models; the kilns were economical and easy to operate. Dinnerwares and fancy items, designed with an understanding of

194. The Noritake mustard pot, green M-in-Wreath mark, has a well-painted landscape and gold decoration on the cobalt blue underglaze border. Interesting lid and handles. The set of nut dishes bears the M-in-Wreath mark.

195. Demitasse cup and saucer and salt dish, bearing Tree Crest mark (green). Blue border, orange flowers, luster.

Western taste and needs, were manufactured there for export to the United States and Europe.

The Noritake Company was the first in Japan to manufacture dinnerwares for export, and was the leader in the field. Other small companies copied its products, but the only company of any size that produced dinnerwares was the Meito Company, which went out of business during World War II.

A variety of other goods was also produced by the Noritake Company: sanitary ware, insulators, and spark plugs, as well as gypsum; in time separate companies were formed for these products. In 1917 a factory for the exclusive production of sanitary wares was established—it is now known as Toto Ltd.; the insulator division became independent in 1919 and split into two companies in 1936, one for porcelain insulators and the other for spark plugs and chemical porcelain; in 1936, also, the gypsum division became a separate company under the name of Nitto Sekko Kaisha Ltd.

Noritake was the only company allowed to continue production of commercial dinnerware during World War II. The government did not want this skill lost, so every effort was made to continue in spite of all difficulties. The company suffered badly during the bombing, and equipment and records were lost.

For a short period after the war, wares made by the Noritake Company were exported under the R.C., or Rose China, mark, as it was felt that the quality was not worthy of the name Noritake. However, wares can be found with the Noritake mark and "Occupied Japan." At present there are eight Noritake factories in Japan that manufacture dinnerware.

A branch of the Noritake Company, the Okura China factory, produces expensive wares that are processed entirely by hand. This factory was begun as the hobby of Baron Okura. Wares (particularly vases) imported into the United States are marked O.A.C. Noritake (Okura Art China).

The "M" in the famous M-in-Wreath mark stands for the name Morimura; it was used until the Morimura office in New York was closed in 1941. After that, the wreath encircled an "N" for Noritake. Another well-known Noritake mark also associated with the Morimura family is the Tree Crest mark (Ill. 195); the symbol, which is sometimes mistakenly called a wheel, or spoke, is the Japanese character for "tree," and is the crest of the Morimura family.

Noritake wares are of a consistent high quality and have their own style and individuality. Unlike the decoration on much of the Nippon ware of the same period, the motifs on Noritake ware were mostly used in the European fashion of decoration.

As the company did both body and

196. The syrup pot and its underplate are richly decorated in gold; porcelain is of excellent quality. The small covered box on pedestal has gold beading with pink rosebuds on a turquoise background. H. 2½". All have R. C. Noritake mark.

decoration, the quality of the two on a single piece are comparable. Nippon, on the other hand, can have fine decoration on a poor body, and vice versa. Noritake decoration often echoed the shape, as it did in the lemon-shaped dish in Ill. 198, and the shapes of the pieces were also individual to the company. Even if a corresponding piece is found with a Nippon mark, the dimensions will be different. This is important to remember when looking at an unmarked piece that might be part of a set; if the dimensions are

not the same as those of a corresponding piece marked Nippon, the piece in question is very likely Noritake.

Although all Noritake wares are made from high quality paste and the bodies are well finished, the finest pieces are those bearing the old R.C. mark—these wares date from about 1911, and at that time the R.C. stood for Royal Ceramic. They were intended to be worthy to compete with the best European porcelain. The molds used were of distinctive shapes, and very often,

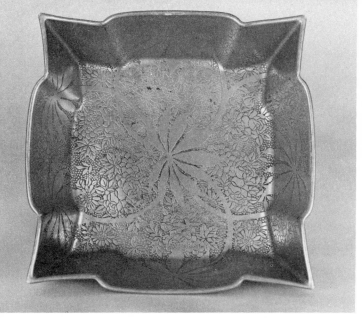

197. Gold Noritake dish with green M-in-Wreath mark. The stamp used to decorate this piece must have had its design etched with acid to produce a surface of this kind. Mrs. Robert Seekamp

198. The spoon holder at left in the group photograph is decorated with pink roses. The two center dishes, both decorated with luster, have a handle formed out of the body; the smaller of the two is not only lemon-shaped but decorated with a lemon. The larger one has a floral motif and a black and gold border. The condiment set at right with azalea decoration and the larger dish are both Noritake green M-in-Wreath; others are red M-in-Wreath. The bowl shown separately, also green M-in-Wreath, has two handles pierced from the body.

199. Although this footed dish carries the green Noritake M-in-Wreath mark, it was probably a blank sent elsewhere for decoration. The floral spray is signed A. Haruno.

after a piece was taken from the mold, it was further shaped by hand. The saucer under the gold-decorated syrup pot in Ill. 196 received this treatment. When a piece like this is held one can feel exactly how the potter manipulated it between his fingers and thumb.

Wares with the old R.C. mark are finely decorated, often with considerable gold-work in excellent taste. The extreme whiteness of the porcelain and the intricate gold decoration combine to give an appearance of great refinement.

In Nippon ware the main interest was in the enameled decoration, but in Noritake the individual shape of the body is often the predominant feature. Frequently a handle is formed out of the body, or openings are made to give a handlelike effect (Ill. 198).

During the first two decades of the twentieth century, the production of blanks to be exported "in the white" for amateur decoration overseas was an important part of the Noritake Company's trade (Ill. 199). The hand painting of china was then a popular way of making a personal gift to a friend, and even complete sets were so decorated and often accompanied by an embroidered matching tray cloth or tablecloth. A semicircular mark with the words "Noritake Nippon" generally was used on these blanks when they were exported to the United States, and pieces with this mark are quite common, with a variety of styles of decoration on them. Some pieces with this mark were sent to other parts of Japan for decoration. On these the Noritake Nippon mark is often seen together with a Nippon symbol, or Japanese characters reading "Kutani" on the same piece (Ill. 200). As the Noritake Company made use of the jigger very early in the history of the company, the manufacture and export of large quantities of blanks was easy.

The Noritake pictorial style of decoration falls roughly into two categories: the

200. The cup and saucer decorated in Kutani style are marked with a semicircular "Noritake Nippon" as well as Japanese characters reading "Kutani" on a red brushstroke. The syrup pitcher has the same semicircular mark, along with the Nippon Maple Leaf mark; it is decorated in gold with turquiose "jewels."

beautifully painted, naturalistic kind, and the stylized (Ill. 201). One type of decoration in the naturalistic style consists of landscapes (Ill. 202); very often a sunset is included, and if it is painted on a set, each piece has a different portion of it, so that if all the pieces are put side by side, the complete scene is encompassed.

In contrast to Nippon ware, which with few exceptions used asymmetrical decoration, Noritake prefers the European symmetrical style. Even when bouquets are painted as natural flowers, they are still used in a rigid pattern and repeated exactly as on European pieces (Ill. 198). A characteristic feature of these bouquet patterns is the use of a kind of shadow painting of a circle of leaves around the bouquet. Another feature is the use, for contrast in bouquets, of one blue *kikyo* flower (bellflower).

The stylized form of decoration, a very distinctive feature of Noritake ware, is generally used on the more commercial lines of wares. Flowers, fruit, birds, fish, and the like are all portrayed in this style (Ill. 203). Very often they form part of a decalcomania used in conjunction with hand-painted work. The forms are more or less geometric, the flower petals being circles, for example. However, these stylized forms can also be found on superior wares (Ill. 204).

Luster is used a great deal, either for the whole decoration or some part of it. As luster is found mostly on wares bearing the red M-in-Wreath mark, and comparatively rarely on those with the green mark, it would seem as if the process were introduced at about the time the color of the mark was changed (Ill. 206). The Noritake Company says that no record exists of the date of this color change, but as the luster process was introduced after the end of the Nippon period (1921), this would place the transition from green mark to red in the mid-twenties, making the green mark the earlier of the two.

201. *The gold-handled basket has beautifully painted floral decoration; Noritake green M-in-Wreath mark. The dresser set, which carries the Tree Crest mark in green, has stylized floral decorations: pink double cherry blossoms, red and blue plum blossoms, gold leaves, and a blue luster border.*

202. *Scalloped-edge dish has three small landscapes, all different. Mark is Noritake Tree Crest in a circle. There is lavish use of gold and green, and a magenta border.* Pinney Collection

203. Examples of Noritake stylized decoration, all with the red M-in-Wreath mark: plate with fruit and flowers; sugar and creamer with flowers and luster; berry set decorated with bowls of fruit. Mr. and Mrs. T. J. Lotito

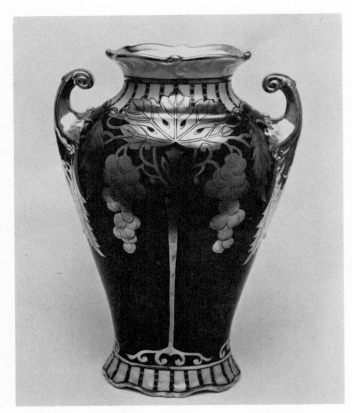

204. Noritake vase, green M-in-Wreath mark, has stylized gold grape decoration on a black ground. The vine even has a stylized root. Note the symmetrical bunches of grapes.

205. Sugar and creamer with allover luster; red M-in-Wreath mark.

206. *The bowl with stylized decoration of fish and birds bears the green M-in-Wreath mark. The identically sized bowl with luster decoration has the same green M-in-Wreath mark, but the third bowl (with luster decoration) bears a red M-in-Wreath mark. The coloring on the second and third bowls is very similar.*

17

Made in Japan (1921-1940)

The mark "Made in Japan" covers wares made in all parts of Japan. These pieces were produced after 1921, when the word "Nippon" was no longer acceptable to the United States government for country of origin. After that time wares were variously marked "Japan" or "Made in Japan," either stamped on the piece or on a paper sticker attached to it.

Many of these export pieces were made in the Seto (Ill. 207) and Nagoya areas, but there was also considerable production in Arita. Pieces made in these areas were sent to decorating studios elsewhere to be finished; Tokyo was a large center for this kind of work. Kaga was another district that special-

ized in decoration, although kilns there also made the biscuit (Ill. 208).

The "Made in Japan" group presents the largest variety of styles and quality of workmanship, the pieces ranging from excellent to very poor. However, I would like to caution against saying "bad" too quickly. There was a lot of hasty work, but that does not always make a piece totally unacceptable. Quite often such a piece has a certain charm or individuality about it. Of course, there was a tremendous quantity of unquestionably poor quality work, but one should not pass judgment too blindly.

Many pieces carry no mark at all; either they came as part of a set in which only

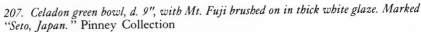

207. *Celadon green bowl, d. 9", with Mt. Fuji brushed on in thick white glaze. Marked "Seto, Japan."* Pinney Collection

208. *The three cups and saucers with Kaga-style decoration have red brown borders. The six-cup chocolate set is decorated mostly with decalcomania, but the added enamel work is well done. Dots of raised enamel represent the blossoms on the trees. This set is better quality than many of its type. Marked "Made in Japan."* Mr. and Mrs. T. J. Lotito

209. *The demitasse set with tray is marked "Kokura, Japan." It has pink, orange, and blue flowers, with green leaves; a black and white border. Good quality porcelain.* Mr. and Mrs. Frank Petta. *The condiment set with an Egyptian scene is marked "Camel China." The decoration on this set is not of such good quality as on the demitasse set; it looks hastily done, and on one piece the head of the rider is missing. However, the set is attractive, and the metal stand, which looks like a kind of silver, has an impressed mark on it that, on cursory inspection, might be taken as an English hallmark, but is not.*

210. Coffeepot, unmarked, has a luster surface with a slip-trailed dragon; gold on handle and lid.

some of the pieces were marked, or they had paper stickers that were soon lost. We have to form our own opinion as to the country of origin. Sometimes this is an easy decision to make, but at other times it is almost impossible to be sure. The problem is further complicated when we have to contend with pieces that were sent out "in the white" for decoration.

In the early part of this century, not only was china painting a popular pastime; there were also any number of small studios specializing in selling hand-painted china. The United States imported blanks from many countries—Japan, France, and · Bavaria, to name only a few. Of course, these blanks had to be marked with the country of origin; but blanks from other countries were also sent to Japan for decoration, and those blanks were not always marked, since Japan had no import regulations requiring such marking (Ill. 211).

Certain wares bear other marks besides "Japan." These fall into two categories: either Japanese characters giving the name of the kiln, company, or potter, or symbols that are descendants of the Nippon marks. The latter, like the Nippon symbols, were mainly export marks, the wares being collected by an agent and shipped abroad, mostly to the United States. Again, like the Nippon symbols, they are of little use to the collector, one symbol being affixed to a wide variety of wares. During the transition period of

211. Although the decoration on this dish (13") appears to be Japanese, quite possibly the body was made elsewhere. It is a very light piece, and the frilled edge suggests the appearance of an Austrian blank. Unmarked.

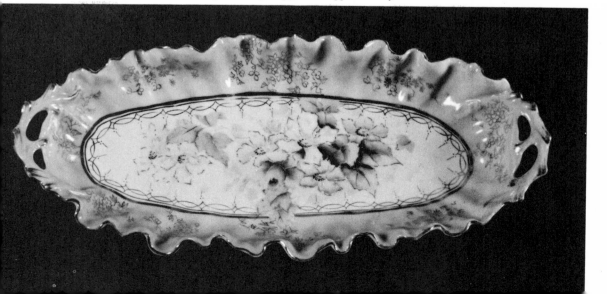

212. *This demitasse set is of excellent quality.* Mrs. Diane Needleman. *The tiny bowl with cream-colored crackled glaze in Satsuma style is marked, in Japanese characters, with the name of the small company that made it.* Pinney Collection

213. *Kaga pieces with very blotchy decoration.*

change from "Nippon" to "Japan," some wares carry both names.

As a rough-and-ready rule, one might say that if there is some mark besides the word "Japan," this implies a better quality, the makers not hiding under the anonymity of "Japan." Pieces bearing Japanese characters are usually of good quality (Ill. 212). However, this does not mean that pieces marked "Made in Japan" are necessarily of poor quality; after all, Japanese potters traditionally do not sign their wares, so a piece imported into the Unites States would be marked only "Made in Japan." The cormorant (Ill. 128) in the Metropolitan Museum of Art is stamped "Made in Japan" on its base. On the other hand, Kaga pieces usually carry a symbol or the name of the small factory in Japanese characters, and much poor quality ware has come from there (Ill. 213).

In the 1920s many imitations of the earlier Nippon and pre-Nippon pieces were made (Ill. 214). As a copy generally lacks the artistic vision of the piece as a whole, the effect is less artistic than on the original, and the piece is lifeless.

The teapot in Ill. 215 is a good example of pre-Nippon style that has lost much of the original fineness. At first it appears to be a very pretty piece, with pink roses on a green enamel background and gold border decoration on underglaze blue. The finial, however, is clumsy and entirely covered with gold, instead of having a gold pattern painted on the underglaze blue; the finial shows blue underneath where the gold has worn off, so no doubt the original intention was to have a gold pattern on the blue, but this was not carried out. The handle is too heavy and ornate, obviously a copy of a handle from some other piece, as it simply does not go artistically with the rest of the teapot. The roses do not have the shaded detail of the earlier pre-Nippon period (1868–1890); white enamel outlines are relied on to mark the petals and shape the flowers. The leaves are done in the same style, with gold outlines on dabs of green paint. Nevertheless, it is still a colorful piece even if it is not up to the standard of the original style.

The tray in Ill. 217 relies rather heavily on its coloring, which unfortunately cannot be seen in a black and white illustration. It

214. *This piece in the shape of a ship's decanter is obviously a copy of a much older piece. On the original the elaborate decoration would have been slip-trailed, but here it was done with thick enamel. The detail photograph shows that the brushwork is not of the fine quality of turn-of-the-century wares. Unmarked.*

215. Teapot made in the 1920s imitating pre-Nippon wares. See Ill. 149 for detail.

216. Scalloped bowl with three feet, 1920s. The brushwork on this piece is similar to that on the teapot in Ill. 215, but as this bowl is of an unpretentious nature, the decoration blends well with the style of potting. "Made in Japan."

217. Another unpretentious "Made in Japan" piece. Decoration is violets and green leaves.

looks as if a child might have painted it, and indeed a child could have, as children have always helped with the decorating in Japan.

Some Nippon marks were retained on "Made in Japan" pieces with very little change. The best example of this is the Torii mark. It remained exactly the same; "Nippon" was simply changed to "Made in Japan." The pieces are often identical too, and one has to turn a piece upside down to see which mark it bears (see Ills. 187 and 191).

Kaga wares retain much of their separate identity. Torii wares were derived from the red Kaga wares of the late nineteenth century, and the same style of decoration was used with the "Made in Japan" marking (Ill. 218).

Another Kaga mark is the T-in-Cherry-Blossom, which, like the Nippon marks, was an export mark. The cherry blossom is the crest of the Maeda family, lords of Kaga. As wares were shipped "in the white" to Kaga

218. *The set with Kaga-style decoration showing a man on horseback crossing a bridge is of only medium quality. The other set, featuring a landscape with Mt. Fuji, is good quality porcelain and decoration. Both are unmarked.* Mr. and Mrs. T. J. Lotito

219. *The handleless cup of wheel-turned gray porcelain has a landscape in underglaze blue applied by transfer. Mark: T-in-Cherry-Blossom, Japan. The decalcomania decoration on the small dish must have been applied before the body was very hard, as the edges were not folded over until after it had been put on. Unmarked.* Pinney Collection

Province for decoration, often acting as ballast on returning ships that had carried rice on their outward journey, a wide variety of wares carry this mark. Some pieces are of good quality porcelain, often decorated in Kutani style (Ill. 153) and probably sent from Arita to Kaga for decoration. Some are in the coarse gray porcelain associated with Kaga wares, and can be found with blue underglaze transfer decoration in Kaga style (Ill. 219).

Probably the most important development of the period was luster decoration. This came in after the Nippon period (1891–1921), and Noritake has used it extensively. These pieces rely on their sheen and coloring for decorative effect. In many cases the brushwork is rather hastily done, but the general effect of the colors is pleasing. The shapes are usually quite commercial and unpretentious (Ill. 220).

One very obvious way in which pro-

220. These salt dishes with landscapes in the center have on orange luster border with gold cherry blossoms. Mark: "Made in Japan," with paulownia leaves.

221. "Made in Japan" chocolate set of mediocre quality. The handles are poorly molded and clumsy, and the enamel decoration poorly done.

222. *Three types of Chinese-style decoration: The plate, d. 10", has a yellow border, pink peonies, and black background. "Made in Japan." The teapot, h. 5½", has red, black, blue, and green panels, a red border on the shoulder, and a black spout. Handle is bamboo. "Made in Japan." The pair of vases, h. 6½ ", have green background. Decoration is mainly a transfer in blue, yellow, and red; clouds are green and black enamel. There is a hand-painted gold line around the base, and neck decoration in red, black, and gold—all careful work, but not much of it. Mark: "Made in Japan" with paulownia leaves.*

223. *Underglaze blue decoration. On the cup and saucer is a dragon design with Chinese-style flames. The dish is decorated with a Hō-ō bird (phoenix) and chrysanthemum and paulownia design; decoration of this kind is popularly called "Flying Turkey." All are marked "Made in Japan."*

224. *Nippon-style vase, h. 9", has Plum Blossom mark and "Hand Painted, Japan." The landscape, which continues around the back, does not have much detail but relies on a few bold brushstrokes. The raised gold decoration is on a shaded brown background; dark green on neck, light green handles.*

225. *Satsuma-style incense burner (b. 8") and bowl, with separate photograph showing the inside of the bowl. Decoration was done with polychrome enamels and a good deal of gold against a black background. The inside of the bowl is an interesting mixture of bas-relief and enamel decoration. Unmarked.*

226. The plate at top is "Thousand Faces" design—each face is slightly different. The plate with "rice" border has a heavily printed decoration in underglaze blue and a very thick glaze. The demitasse cup and saucer are decorated in orange and gold. All these pieces are marked "Made in Japan," but the fourth photograph shows an unmarked plate, cup, and saucer in fine porcelain.

227. The set shown here, with slip-trailed dragons and airbrush design, is unmarked, but an attached paper sticker reads: "Betson, Japan." Mr. and Mrs. T. M. Lotito. The Satsuma-style dark brown vase is also unmarked, but the Imari-style plate is marked "Made in Japan."

duction costs were cut to the detriment of the finished product was including the handles in the mold instead of making them separately and attaching them to the body with slip. Handles made in this way are much heavier and not so clean-cut. The method of manufacture is immediately apparent if one looks inside a piece. If handle and body were molded in the same mold, porcelain was drawn up into the handle, making a hollow at this point inside the body. If the handle was attached with slip, the body is smooth inside.

A vast quantity of various types of ceramics bears the words "Made in Japan," ranging from pottery to faience to porcelain. Some are good, some are bad. The collector must rely on his own judgment and taste, and have the courage of his convictions.

Form your own opinions rather than listen to the next person, unless you have a particular reason to respect his judgment. In this way your own taste will grow, and if it is not the same as your neighbor's, who is to say that his taste is better than yours? At least you will have your own reasons for liking what you like, and you will not be a poor copy of what you imagine you should be.

Figurines were manufactured by the thousands in the 1921–1940 period, and many were made after Austrian and German models. Usually they are distinguishable from the European ones because they have a brighter gold. The china is of a different quality as well—it is softer, and the wares do not feel as sharp as the Austrian ones.

Satsuma-style and Imari wares have been dealt with elsewhere, and pieces with slip-trailed dragons are mentioned in the discussion of Nippon. All these wares became widely mass-produced and are generally less pleasing than the earlier examples (Ill. 227).

228. The small vases and cherub figurine (h. 4") are marked "Made in Japan." The Toby mug and the dish are both marked "Japan." The Toby has a decided oriental slant to the eyes. Mr. and Mrs. T. J. Lotito

18

Occupied Japan (1945–1952) and Later

The Occupation of Japan lasted for six and a half years. It was the first time in her long history that Japan had come under the control of foreign conquerors.

The war left behind a tremendous amount of devastation. Most factories had either been destroyed or else were closed for lack of materials. Japan's foreign markets were gone and her merchant marine, necessary to transport goods for foreign trade, was nonexistent. With the aid of the Americans, however, the Japanese worked hard at clearing the devastation and reviving their economic life.

A great variety of ceramic wares was produced during the Occupation period, especially chinaware, both for sale to GIs stationed there and for export. Some is of fine quality, some rather crude, and some, to say the least, peculiar.

Cups and saucers rank high in the better class of wares. Some were made from a good fine porcelain and have tasteful decoration. Cups can be found in a wide array of shapes: the small friendship variety for gift giving, demitasse cups, coffee cups, teacups, cups in English, French, and German styles, cups with various Japanese styles of decoration,

229. *Occupied Japan pieces: The cup and saucer on opposite page have a black background and are marked "Made in Occupied Japan" and with C-in-Wreath. The creamer at top left is not well done, but the work on the other two pieces is good; creamer and cup are marked "Made in Occupied Japan"; the plate has "Ironstone Ware" added as well. At top right, the little friendship cup and saucer, marked "Ohashi China, Occupied Japan," have pink and orange flowers alternating with gold medallions against a dark green background.* Pinney Collection. *In the group of three demitasse cups and saucers, at center right, the one at the left is marked "Hand Painted" and "Gold China, Occupied Japan"; the center one decorated by decalcomania is marked "Fuji China, Occupied Japan"; the one at right, hand painted, reads "Made in Occupied Japan." At bottom right, the German-style cup and saucer are marked "Gold Castle, Occupied Japan"; the demitasse beside it, simply "Made in Occupied Japan."*

230. "Occupied Japan" pieces of very good quality: The plate, d. 9½", is in the Chinese style, with cobalt blue background, yellow tree, pink and white plum blossoms, red, pink, and white peonies. The cup and saucer are decorated in black and brown. The miniature coffee set on a 3½" tray has fine decoration consisting of gold flowers and enamel beading on a green background; the flower basket is blue. All are marked "Made in Occupied Japan," but on the cup and saucer the word "Hokutacha" is added also.

231. *Figurines in European style: The two at top left, h. 7½", have green and brown costumes in muted tones.* Mrs. C. Howell. *The two above, h. 6", are dressed in green and have gold highlights. The couple at lower left, an unusually tall piece (12"), were probably inspired by a European print. All are marked "Made in Occupied Japan."*

232. *The figurine (h. 5½") of a boy playing a violin may well have been inspired by the popular Hummel figures. Decoration is in warm browns and orange; black hat and umbrella. Marked "Made in Japan."* Mr. and Mrs. T. J. Lotito. *The figurines in the large group, perhaps also Hummel-inspired, are 4½" high and marked "Made in Occupied Japan."*

233. *Group of four imitation "German" beer mugs with incised German words are all marked "Made in Japan." Mrs. C. Howell. The other two mugs, with less detail and fuzzy decoration, are very light ware marked "Made in Occupied Japan."*

cups decorated mainly on the outside, and cups decorated mainly on the inside. All these, of course, have corresponding saucers (Ill. 229).

By far the largest group of "Occupied Japan" articles is the figurines. They were made in every imaginable shape: figures in European period costume (Ill. 231); in Chinese or Japanese costume; figures playing oriental and European instruments; dancing figures, sailor boys, Dutch girls, mermaids, elves, babies, cherubs, and so on (Ill. 232). There were also animals of all kinds, frogs, swans, and all sorts of birds, as well as baby booties, horse-drawn carriages, and other objects (Ill. 234). In my personal opinion, the figurines of groups of oriental dancers and instrumentalists are the most colorful and interesting.

It seems to me that the better wares usually followed a form of traditional Japanese or Chinese style. Many of the souvenir type of wares appear to have been modeled on the inferior export wares of the twenties and thirties. There are also extraordinary oddities that no doubt were intended to please the resident GI but did not quite come off.

As far as marks are concerned, a great many different ones are in existence, although, of course, many pieces are just stamped "Made in Occupied Japan." I do not know how many different marks there are, but I would hazard a guess at around seventy-five or more, and this may be a conservative estimate. I have even seen a mark saying that the piece was made in Occupied Japan and designed somewhere in Florida. This struck me as exceedingly strange—al-

234. The pianist and her piano are marked "Made in Occupied Japan." The assortment of doll furniture, quite poorly made, is marked either "Japan" or "Made in Japan."

though the Japanese may have needed help financially, or with materials; surely they had no problem in designing chinaware. Perhaps the Japanese decorator merely wished to carry out an American design in order to make his wares acceptable for the American market. Interestingly enough, the piece was decorated with a very ordinary landscape of the kind that was done much better on Nippon pieces.

Recently, fake pieces of "Occupied Japan" have come on the market. These are much lighter in weight than the originals, and have a thin soft body that is hollow inside. They carry a mark written in script, either in orange or black on those I have seen so far. However, as they do not have the feel of the originals, no serious collector should have trouble differentiating between the two wares.

Since the end of the Occupation the export of Japanese ceramics has again become a flourishing industry. Excellent quality dinnerwares are in plentiful supply and fancy porcelains are available, as well as peasant-type wares.

Besides the traditional Imari, Kutani, and Satsuma wares, other wares in traditional styles are being produced and exported. In the Arita area the Fukagawa Porcelain Manufacturing Company makes very fine porcelain with decoration in beautiful colors (Ill. 236). Happu folk wares are made in the Isé district and exported abroad in large quantities (Ill. 237). They are made in the local tradition from regional clays.

In conclusion, I hope that this book will have stimulated interest in the enormous variety of wares available to collectors of Japanese ceramics, and the basic information provided will enable readers to move on to more detailed books on the subject.

Because of the scarcity of Japanese written records much controversy exists over dates, kilns, and potters. However, rather than deterring collectors, this should give them an added incentive to form their own collections, and draw their own conclusions as to the correctness of available information. With this in mind, study collections of imperfect wares can be made, and a great deal of firsthand knowledge can be obtained at a very moderate cost.

235. *Satsuma-style cup and saucer with Satsuma crest (cross in circle); inside of cup is gold luster. "Made in Occupied Japan."*

236. Covered bowl made by the Fukagawa Porcelain Manufacturing Company (established 1689) is excellent quality porcelain with delicate hand-painted gold decoration on cobalt blue background.

Appendix of Marks and Periods

Jōmon Period: c. 4500 B.C.–c. 200 B.C.
Yayoi Period: c. 200 B.C.–A.D. 250
Kofun Period: 250–552
Asuka Period: 552–646
Nara Period: 646–794
Heian Period: 794–1185

Kamakura Period: 1185–1333
Muromachi Period: 1333–1568
Momoyama Period: 1568–1615
Edo Period: 1615–1868
Meiji Period: 1868–1912
Taisho Period: 1912–1926

Showa Period: 1926–present day

道八製　大日本
Dōhachi

清風造　大日本
Seifû

帯山製　大日本
Tanzan

日本吉　太田造
Banko

造山光錦都京本日
Kinkozan

fuku, *good luck*

R.C. Nippon

M-in-Wreath

Maple Leaf

Imperial

S.N.B. Nagoya

Pointed Crown

Pagoda

Royal Satsuma

Torii

O.A.C. Nippon

Square Crown

S & K Nippon

200

R.C. Noritake

T-in-Wreath

M-in-Wreath Noritake

The Yamato Nippon

Tree-Crest Noritake

Cherry Blossom

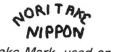

Noritake Mark, used on blanks

T.S. Nippon

Tree-Crest Nippon

HAND PAINTED NIPPON

Paulownia Blossom

Rising Sun   Plum Blossom   Cherry Blossom

Glossary

aburazara: oil dish

aka-: red

aka-e: "red painted" (red pictures). Japanese term for overglaze or polychrome enamels

aka-e machi: "street of enamelers." Arita street, founded in seventeenth century, where Imari ware was decorated and sold

akaji-kinga: gold designs on red

Amakusa stone: a form of semidecomposed feldspar found in Kyushu

ana-gama: "cellar kiln." A single-chamber sloping kiln, first used by the Chinese and introduced into Japan by Korean potters

ao-: "green"; e.g., Ao-Kutani, Ao-Oribe

arabesque: a florid style of ornament developed by Arabian art workers; usually composed of scrolls and floral tracery

Arita ware: porcelain ware produced in Arita; includes Imari, Kakiemon, Nabeshima, and Hirado wares

ash glaze: glaze produced from wood ash falling on the ware in the kiln during firing

aubergine: a deep purple color like the skin of the eggplant

Awata ware: earthenware, or faience, decorated with overglaze enamel

bail handle: a hoop-shaped handle extending over the top from one side to the other

ball clay: a plastic secondary clay that fires white and withstands high temperatures in the kiln

bank kiln: a sloping kiln, the slope taking the place of a chimney

bento-bako: tiered lunch boxes

biscuit: pottery or porcelain that has been fired once but has not been glazed

blue and white ware: white porcelain with decoration in underglaze blue

body: the clay of which a pot is made

bone china: English soft porcelain composed of approximately one part ox-bone ash, one part china clay (kaolin), and one part Cornish stone (petuntse). The addition of bone ash causes vitrification to take place at a relatively low temperature.

brocade: Any mass of bright colors is called a brocade by the Japanese. See *nishikide*

casting: making shapes by pouring liquid clay into plaster molds

celadon: *seiji* in Japanese. The French name for a large family of oriental porcelain and stonewares with soft green crackled glaze. The general explanation for the word was the similarity of the color of the ware to the green ribbons worn by Céladon, the hero of the novel *L'Astrée*, by Honoré d'Urfé. Another explanation is that it was derived from the name of Sultan Sālāh-ed-din (Saledin), who made a gift of forty pieces of celadon to the Sultan of Damascus in 1171.

cha: tea

chajin: tea master

cha-no-yu: Japanese tea ceremony

cha-wan: teabowl

china: a term used for soft-paste porcelains in general

china clay: a form of kaolin, less plastic than that found in China and Japan

Ching-tê-chên: site of imperial Chinese porcelain factories

Chōsen: Korea

clay: semidecomposed feldspar, ground into particles, with the soluble elements removed

cloisonné: enamel decoration set in hollows formed by thin strips of wire welded to a metal plate

cobalt oxide: the coloring agent for almost all blues

Cochin chinaware: see Kōchi-*yaki*

coil building: forming the walls of pots with ropes of clay

Cornish stone: a semidecomposed feldspar, similar but not identical to petuntse

cover finial: a protuberance on the top of the lid or cover of a tureen, sugar bowl, teapot, vase, or the like, by which the cover may be lifted

crackle: intentional network of fine cracks on the surface of a glaze

crazing: an unintentional and faulty crackling of a glaze, caused by the thermal expansion and contraction of the glaze being different from that of the clay body

daimyo: lord

dampers: adjustable shutters used to control the draft in a kiln *dobin:* a ceramic teapot or hot-water kettle with bail handle

doki: "earthen vessel." Japanese term for low-fired pottery

drape mold (or flopover mold): a mold in the shape of the interior contour of the ware

drying: removal of water from the clay. The water added to clay in the formation of the ware is eliminated by the time the firing has reached 212°F.; the chemically combined water that is part of the composition of the clay is driven off at temperatures between about 675° and 1,300°F. After this the clay cannot be reclaimed, as it has undergone a chemical change.

e-: painted; e.g., *E*-Shino, "painted Shino"

earthenware: all glazed wares with a porous body

Edo: old name for Tokyo

eggshell porcelain: a name given to very thin translucent Japanese or Chinese export porcelain

egote: stick used to shape the inside of tall pieces on the wheel

enamels: low temperature colored glazes applied over harder glazes. These are fired at a lower temperature than the harder glaze, and adhere to the glaze without mixing with it.

engobe: slip used to coat the entire surface of a piece, changing its color

faience: a French name loosely applied to glazed earthenware in general

Famille verte, noire, and rose: French names given by the French historian of pottery, Albert Jacquemart (1808–1875), to three classes of Chinese porcelain

feldspar: an opaque white crystal found in granite, which melts between about 2,200° and 2,375°F. It is extensively used for ceramic bodies and glazes.

fettling: the process of smoothing the surface of leather-hard clay

finial: see cover finial

firing: the burning or stoking of a kiln

foot: the expansion at the base (generally circular) of the stem of a vessel, which it stands on

frits: a finely ground glassy substance widely used in the manufacture of commercial glazes

fude: Japanese painting and writing brush; *dami-fude,* large brush used for large washes of color

fuku: Japanese character meaning good fortune or blessing

fusible clays: clays that vitrify and lose their shape at or below 2,200°F.; used in the Orient for stoneware glazes

glost firing: glaze firing

goma: glaze caused by ash falling on the ware during firing; the "sesame seed" effect of Bizen ash glaze

gosu: natural cobalt found in pebble form in oriental creek beds. The term *gosu* is used to distinguish Japanese porcelains decorated in Chinese Ming style from *sometsuke,* the ordinary blue and white wares

gosu-aka-e: overglaze red and green decoration, sometimes with underglaze blue

grain-de-riz: French term for wares decorated with carving in shape of rice grains, filled in with transparent glaze

greenware: unfired pottery

grog: powdered burnt fireclay

hachi-ho: symbols of the Chinese Eight Treasures: the coin, books, stone chime, artemisia leaf, pearl, lozenge, mirror, and rhinoceros horns

hake: wide flat brush with short bristles

hakeme: broomlike brush made from tips of rice stalks or similar material; "brush-grain" decoration

hakudei ware: "white clay." Unglazed burnished ware of Tokoname

hanakago-de: flower basket pattern, showing a wicker basket, usually with a high loop handle, filled with flowers; popular on Imari wares

haniwa: "clay circles." Kofun Period (552 B.C.–A.D. 250) pottery figures and cylindrical forms, which were placed around burial mounds

happo: same as *hachi-ho*

hard paste porcelain: porcelain made from a mixture of china clay, feldspar, and other natural materials, which is fired at over 2,375°F.

hari-awase: "pasting together"; building with clay slabs

hari-tsuke: "sticking on"; a type of appliqué

Heian: old name for Kyoto. Heian Period (794–1185)

hera: bamboo knife or spatula

herame: spatula marks (on tea ceremony wares)

hidasuki: "fire-cord" effect. This was traditional decoration on Bizen ware, made by wrapping the wares with cords made of straw soaked in salt water, before firing. During the firing the straw burns away, depositing the sodium from the salt on the surface of the ware. The sodium combines with the red clay and causes bright red streaks of glaze to appear on the otherwise unglazed surface.

himo-tsukuri: "coil-building"

hiragana: see *kana*

Hō-ō bird: variously translated as phoenix or bird of paradise; the design originally came from China. The Hō-ō motif is associated with the empress of Japan, and is usually pictured with the empress's crest, the leaves of the paulownia tree *(kiri-no-mon).*

hori-dashi: "carving-out" a form from a single clay block

Imari ware: Arita porcelain wares for domestic and export use (excluding Kakiemon, Nabeshima, and Hirado wares) shipped from the port of Imari

impermeable: waterproof; bodies that have become nonporous through vitrification

iro-: "color"; e.g., Iro-Nabeshima

iro-gawari: Ryumonji transparent glaze

iron: a most useful coloring agent for clay, pigments, and glazes, as it withstands high temperatures. In the lower temperatures it gives yellows, browns, reds, and blacks; with higher temperatures, greens, blues, browns, and blacks.

ironstone china: a fine hard earthenware

jigger: a modern mechanical device for forming dinnerware commercially at high speed. It consists of an adjustable arm, which holds a profile that presses soft clay either into or onto a revolving plaster mold.

jiu, also *ju:* the Chinese symbol for longevity

Jōmon: "rope pattern," the oldest prehistoric Japanese earthenware. The name is derived from the impressed rope and cord decoration.

ju: see *jiu*

kachō: flower and bird design

Kaga Province: modern Ishikawa Prefecture

Kaga ware: a general term for ceramics made in Kaga Province

kaki: "persimmon"

kama: kiln

kana: the Japanese syllabary, derived from certain Chinese characters, greatly abbreviated, used as phonetic symbols. Each symbol represents one monosyllabic word or syllable, in contrast to the alphabet, which represents single sounds. These symbols are written in two different ways: *hiragana* and *katakana. Hiragana:* the whole character is written in stylized or cursive form. *Katakana:* an element of the character stands for the phonetic value of the whole.

kanna: "planes"

kaolin: anglicized form of the Chinese word for china clay, Kao-ling, "the high hills." It was named after the hills near Ching-te-Chen, where it was excavated.

Kara: china

karakō: "Chinese children" decoration

Karatsu: "China port"

kasasa: feldspar

kasuri-mon: chatter-mark decoration

katakana: see *kana*

ke-rokuro: "kick wheel"

kezuri: "trimming"

kezuri no dōgu: "trimming tools"

ki-: yellow

kikai rokuro: jigger wheel

Kiyomizu-*yaki:* wares decorated with overglaze enamels, produced in the vicinity of the Kiyomizu temple, Kyoto. The modern (post-1868) term for Kyoto wares, as opposed to the Edo Period term Kyō-*yaki*

ki-zeto: yellow Seto ware

kinrande: porcelain decoration in red and gold, based on Chinese prototypes

ko-: old. *Ko-zeto,* old Seto

Kōchi-*yaki* (Chinese Cochin ware): wares decorated in green and other colored glazes separated by low relief decoration. Originally produced in South China

koge: "scorch marks," found on Iga and Oribe wares

Koku-Ho, Law of: "national treasures." Okakura was responsible for the enactment of this law in 1884; it required all remaining objects of ancient Japanese art to be registered and restricted from export.

kuchi-beni: "mouth rouge"; the line of iron red glazing around Kakiemon wares

kuro-: black. Kuro-Raku, black Raku

kushi: "comb"

kushi-de: the "comb-mark" decoration found on the foot of Nabeshima wares.

After the Meiji Restoration the design was also used by other kilns.

kushime: "comb-grain" decoration

Kutani ware: wares named after the remote village in Kaga Province where it was originally produced. Later wares bearing the Kutani mark were made throughout Kaga Province.

Kyoto: "western capital"

Kyō-*yaki:* "capital ware." Monochrome, underglaze, and overglaze decorated wares, following the tradition of Ninsei and Kenzan, produced in the vicinity of Kyoto during the Edo Period

leather-hard: also called "cheese-hard." The stage in the drying process when the ware is no longer plastic, but not yet dry, and cuts like leather or cheese

luster: a form of decoration made by applying a thin skin of certain metals, in liquid form, to the surface of a glaze. This is subsequently fired in a low reducing atmosphere and imparts an iridescent surface to the glaze.

luting: joining together leather-hard surfaces of clay with slip

Maeda family: rulers of Kaga Province in feudal times, who established a kiln believed to be the original Kutani ware kiln

majolica: a corruption of the name Majorca, given to Italian tin-enameled pottery

maku-gusuri: "wavy-welt glaze"; the wavy surface patterns on Raku ware caused by the thick application of the glaze

matcha: "rubbed tea"; finely powdered tea used for the tea ceremony

matt glaze: glaze with dull surface after firing

mingei: "folk art"

mishima: inlaylike decoration, producing designs of contrasting colors

mizusashi: water jar used in the tea ceremony

mukōzuki: small dishes

nagashi-gusuri: "glaze that is made to flow"; superimposed glaze dripping

naze-kawa: chamois-skin swab for dampening clay

neriage: mosaic pattern developed by pressing clays of different colors into a mold; the pattern is the same inside and outside. This process dates from the Sung Dynasty in China.

neutral atmosphere: atmosphere in the kiln halfway between oxidation and reduction

nezumi-: gray. Nezumi Shino, gray Shino

nigoshi-de: milk white porcelain associated with Kakiemon wares

ningen kokuho: "living national treasure"

nishikide: "brocade-style" type of decoration, which covers the whole surface. Associated with the overglaze enamel decoration of the Imari wares of the eighteenth and nineteenth centuries

nobori-gama: "climbing kiln"; a kiln with stepped chambers, introduced into Japan by Korean potters

Old East Indian ware: old English name for Kakiemon ware

open clays: sandy-textured porous clays

oxidation firing: firing the kiln in such a manner that combustion is complete and the burning gases amply supplied with oxygen. This causes the metals in the clay and glaze to give their oxide colors.

petuntse (pai-tun-tzū): semidecomposed feldspar found in China; it is less decomposed than kaolin.

pilgrim bottle: a canteen-shaped vase, flattened on the two opposite sides

porcelain: pottery that is white, vitrified, and translucent, and has been fired at a high temperature (about 2,375°F.)

pottery: wares made of clay and water that have been fired at a heat of about 1,100°F. or more, and have undergone the resulting chemical changes

press molds: molds into which slabs of clay are pressed to form wares

pyrometers: instruments used in kilns for measuring the temperature

Raku-*yaki:* "pleasure wares," a type of light porous ware with crackled lead glaze, much favored for tea ceremony pieces. The name Raku is derived from a seal presented to Jōkei by Hideyoshi.

raw glazes: glazes that can be applied to greenware

reduction firing: firing a kiln in such a way that combustion is incomplete or smoky, and the carbon present reduces the oxides to their respective metals

redwares, or red-painted wares: seventeenth-century Dutch term for Japanese porcelain with blue underglaze and red overglaze enamels (with or without gold), in contrast to "blue" for blue and white wares

refractory materials: materials able to withstand the high temperatures needed to make hard porcelain

rice-grain decoration: see *grain-de-riz*

rokuro: original oriental potter's wheel: *Ke-rokuro*, kick wheel (always turned counterclockwise). *Te-rokuro*, hand wheel (always turned clockwise)

saggars: fireclay boxes used in the kiln; wares were packed in these to protect them from the direct action of the flames

sake bottle: a pottery bottle, often square, for holding sake (rice liquor)

sansai: "three colors." Wares in imitation of the Chinese three-colored glazed pottery of the Tang Dynasty, produced in Japan during the eighth century for the court at Nara. Also called Nara *sansai*

seiji: see celadon

sgraffito: decoration made by scratching through a covering of slip on leather-hard pots to expose the color of the clay below

shibui: "tastefully astringent." An aesthetic term meaning sober, quiet, or unostentatious

shio-gusuri: "salt glaze"

shiro: white

shizumi-botan: "sinking peony"; an incised decoration covered with celadon glaze

slip: clay diluted with water

slip-trailing: a method of decorating leather-hard wares with lines of raised slip. In Japan a bamboo tube was originally used for this, but nowadays the slip is squeezed out of a rubber syringe.

some-nishiki-de: a characteristic Imari ware technique in which the ware is first decorated in underglaze blue and then in overglaze enamel colors

sometsuke: decoration in underglaze blue on white porcelain

split bamboo kiln: a sloping kiln, so-called because it resembles a split stalk of bamboo. Introduced by Korean potters

spurs: triangular clay supports used in saggars for glazed wares

stilts: clay supports used for firing glazed wares

stoneware: an opaque, vitrified, hard substance between pottery and porcelain

tebineri: "hand pinching"

temmoku: a lustrous black iron glaze. The term is derived from the Tien Mu Mountain in Chekiang, where Zen monks first used Chien ware bowls for the tea ceremony. These bowls were later imitated at the Seto kilns.

terra-cotta: low-fired unglazed pottery

throwing: the process of forming wares on the potter's wheel

tombo: "dragonfly"; bamboo tool used to gauge diameter of cups and bowls

tomoe: commalike symbols

trailing: see slip-trailing

treading: the process of kneading clay by the pressure of the bare human heel, still preferred in Japan

turning: shaving leather-hard clay from the walls of pots on a potter's wheel or lathe

uki-botan: "floating peony"; low-relief decoration adopted by Seto potters from Chinese Northern-Sung celadons, covered with a celadon glaze

underglaze decoration: decoration painted directly on the biscuit, then covered with a translucent glaze and fired

unka ware: "cloud flower"; a burnished unglazed ware decorated with carbon impregnation

vitrification: the change into a glasslike substance resulting from fusion due to heat

wax resist: a decorating technique carried out by first covering a piece with a coat of glaze in the desired color for the decoration; then, when this is dry, painting the decoration in wax. Finally, when the wax has hardened, the piece receives a coating of glaze in the color for the background. As the wax prevents the second coat of glaze from sticking to the first coat in the decorated area, when the piece is fired the wax is burnt off and leaves the decoration in the first color.

-yaki: "ware"

yakimono: ceramic ware

yamato-e: Japanese-style decoration of simplicity and blank spaces

zōgan: "inlay" made with strips of contrasting slip set into a carved surface

Bibliography

ADACHI, BARBARA. *The Living Treasures of Japan*. Tokyo, Japan: Kodansha International Ltd., 1973.

BEASLEY, W. G. *Modern History of Japan*. New York and Washington, D.C.: Frederick A. Praeger, 1963.

BENEDICT, RUTH. *The Chrysanthemum and the Sword*. Boston: Houghton Mifflin Co., 1946.

BEURDELEY, MICHEL. *Chinese Trade Porcelain*. Rutland, Vermont: Charles E. Tuttle Co., 1962.

BRINKLEY, CAPTAIN S. *Japan, Its History, Arts and Literature*. Vol. 8, Keramic Art. London, 1904.

BROOKS, VAN WYCK. *Fenollosa and His Circle*. New York: E. P. Dutton & Co., Inc., 1962.

BUHOT, JEAN. *Chinese and Japanese Art*. Garden City, New York: Doubleday & Co., Inc., 1961.

CARDOZA, SIDNEY. *Rosanjin*. New York: Japan Society, Inc., 1972.

CHAFFERS, WILLIAM. *Marks and Monograms on European and Oriental Pottery and Porcelain*. Borden.

Contemporary Ceramic Art of Japan. Japan: Ministry of Foreign Affairs, 1972.

FRANKS, SIR AUGUSTUS W. *Japanese Pottery, Being a Native Report with an Introduction and Catalogue*. London: Wyman & Sons, 1906.

FUJIOKA, RYOICHI. *Tea Ceremony Utensils*. Tokyo, Japan: Weatherhill/Shibundō, 1973.

GARNER, SIR HARRY. *Oriental Blue and White*. New York and London: Pitman, n.d.

GORHAM, HAZEL. *Japanese and Oriental Ceramics*. Rutland, Vermont: Charles E. Tuttle Co., 1971.

HANNOVER, EMIL. *Pottery and Porcelain of the Far East*. Trans. by Bernard Rackham. London, 1925.

HOBSON, R. L. *Handbook of the Pottery and Porcelain of the Far East in the British Museum*. London, 1924.

HONEY, W. B. *The Ceramic Art of China and Other Countries of the Far East*. London, 1945.

HORIOKA, YASUKO. *The Life of Kakuzō*. Tokyo, Japan: The Hokuseido Press, 1963.

Japan Interpreter, The. Vol. 8, No. 1. Tokyo, Japan: The Japan Center for International Exchange, November 1973.

JENYNS, SOAME. *Japanese Porcelain*. New York and Washington, D.C.: Frederick A. Praeger, 1965.

———. *Japanese Pottery*. New York and Washington, D.C.: Frederick A. Praeger, 1971.

JOLY, HENRI L. *Legend in Japanese Art*. Rutland, Vermont: Charles E. Tuttle Co., 1967.

LEACH, BERNARD. *A Potter in Japan*. New York: Transatlantic Arts, Inc., 1967.

———. *A Potter's Book*. New York: Transatlantic Arts, Inc., 1972.

MIKAMI, TSUGIO. *The Art of Japanese Ceramics*. Tokyo, Japan: Weatherhill/Heibonsha, 1972.

MILLER, ROY ANDREW. *Japanese Ceramics*. Tokyo, Japan: Toto Shuppan Co. Ltd., distributed by Charles E. Tuttle Co., Rutland, Vermont, 1960.

MITSUOKA, TADANARI. *Ceramic Art of Japan*. Tokyo, Japan: Japan Travel Bureau, 1956.

MORISON, SAMUEL E. *"Old Bruin," Commodore Matthew Calbraith Perry*. Boston: Little, Brown & Co., 1967.

MORRIS, IVAN. *The World of the Shining Prince*. New York: Alfred A. Knopf, Inc., 1964.

MORSE, EDWARD SYLVESTER. *Catalogue of the Morse Collection of Japanese Pottery*. Boston, 1901.

———. *Japan Day by Day*. Boston: Houghton Mifflin Co., 1916.

———. *Japanese Homes and Their Surroundings*. New York: Dover Publications, Inc., 1961.

MUNSTERBERG, HUGO. *The Ceramic Art of Japan*. Rutland, Vermont: Charles E. Tuttle Co., 1964.

————. *The Folk Arts of Japan.* Rutland, Vermont: Charles E. Tuttle Co., 1958.

OKAKURA, KAKUZO. *The Book of Tea.* Rutland, Vermont: Charles E. Tuttle Co., 1956.

————. *The Ideals of the East, with Special Reference to the Art of Japan.* Rutland, Vermont: Charles E. Tuttle Co., 1970.

Philadelphia, Official Catalogue of the Japanese Section at the International Exhibition. Philadelphia, 1876.

REISCHAUER, EDWIN O. *Japan: The Story of a Nation.* New York: Alfred A. Knopf, Inc., 1970.

RHODES, DANIEL. *Clay and Glazes for the Potter.* Philadelphia: Chilton Book Co., 1957.

————. *Stoneware and Porcelain.* Philadelphia: Chilton Book Co., 1959.

————. *Tamba Pottery.* Tokyo, Japan: Kodansha International Ltd., 1970.

St. Louis, Official Catalogue of the Louisiana Purchase Exhibition. St. Louis, 1904.

San Francisco, Official Catalogue to the Department of Fine Arts at the Panama-Pacific Exposition. San Francisco, 1915.

SANDERS, HERBERT. *The World of Japanese Ceramics.* Tokyo, Japan: Kodansha International Ltd., 1967.

SATO, MASAHIKO. *Kyoto Ceramics.* Tokyo, Japan: Weatherhill/Shibundō, 1973.

Seattle Art Museum. *International Symposium on Japanese Ceramics.* Seattle, 1972.

SITWELL, SACHEVERELL. *The Bridge of the Brocade Sash.* Cleveland and New York: World Publishing Co., 1959.

STATLER, OLIVER. *The Black Ships Scroll.* Rutland, Vermont: Charles E. Tuttle Co., 1963.

STEINBERG, RAFAEL. *Japan.* New York: Macmillan, 1969.

SWANN, PETER. *Art of China, Korea and Japan.* New York and Washington, D.C.: Frederick A. Praeger, 1963.

TURK, FRANK A. *Japanese Objets d'Art.* New York: Sterling Publishing Co., 1962.

WAYMAN, DOROTHY G. *Edward Sylvester Morse.* Cambridge, Massachusetts: Harvard University Press, 1942.

YANAGI, SŌETSU. *The Unknown Craftsman.* Tokyo, Japan: Kodansha International Ltd., 1972.

Index